D1308498

My Second Picture Dictionary

by Hale C. Reid
Helen W. Crane
Betty Ellen Jenkins

Illustrations by Tom Cooke *and* Bea Holmes

Ginn and Company
A XEROX EDUCATION COMPANY

To the Boys and Girls Who Use This Book

Welcome to MY SECOND PICTURE DICTIONARY. This book has two parts. The first part has words and meanings. The second part has lists of special words. Both parts have many colorful pictures.

The first part lists words in alphabetical order. These words are printed in dark type. They are called *entry words*. What are the entry words on page 1?

Beside most entry words is the definition, or meaning. What is the definition for the word **hat** on page 64?

Below the definition for the entry words is a sentence or a group of sentences. The sentences show you ways the entry word can be used. On page 14 read the sentences for the word **boat.**

Some entry words are printed in two or more parts. Each part is called a *syllable*. What are the syllables in the word **today**? In writing you can divide a word between syllables at the end of a line. Where would you divide the word **today** at the end of a line?

Often there is a small mark (') following a syllable. This mark is called a *stress mark*. It shows you which syllable you should speak louder. Where would the stress mark be in the word **today**?

Sometimes an entry word has a direction instead of a definition. Look up the word **ate.** Follow the direction and see what you find. Now look up the word **lion.** What do you find when you follow the direction?

The second part of the dictionary has lists of words. In each list the words are in alphabetical order and are related to one another. Find page 189. What lists follow this page?

We hope that you will enjoy using MY SECOND PICTURE DICTIONARY to learn about words.

The Authors

© Copyright 1976, 1971, 1967, by Ginn and Company (Xerox Corporation)
Home Office, Lexington, Massachusetts 02173
0-663-31523-9

All Rights Reserved

Curr
PE
1629
.R41
1985
text

Contents

Do You Know?

Look at the forms of the letter A at the top of page 1. Do you know the names of the two animals pictured with the letters? With what letter does each animal's name begin? As you use this dictionary, see if you know the names of the other animals and objects shown with the letters at the beginning of each section. The list below will help you review the alphabet and name the pictures.

A a	alligator, ant	
B b	boy, butterfly, balloon	
C c	caterpillar, cap	
D d	donkey, daisies	
E e	elf, Easter egg	
F f	farmer, frog, flowers	
G g	girl, glasses	
H h	hippopotamus, hat	
I i	Indian	
J j	jack-in-the-box	
K k	kangaroo, kite	
L l	lion, lorgnette	
M m	moose, mirror	

N n	newsboy, newspapers
O o	octopus, orchid
P p	parrot
Q q	question mark
R r	rooster, robin
S s	sailor, soda, straw
T t	tiger, trumpet
U u	unicorn, umbrella
V v	violinist
W w	walrus, watch
X x	xylophone
Y y	yak, yo-yo
Z z	zebra, zinnia

a
any; one
Do you have **a** dollar?
A sunny day makes me feel happy.

about
having to do with; almost; around
Bill wrote a story **about** animals.
The time is **about** two o'clock.
The boat bounced **about** on the lake.

above
higher than; over
The red books are **above** the blue books in the bookcase.
Our apartment is **above** a store.

across
on the other side of; from one side to the other
The city is **across** the river.
The dog ran **across** the road.

afraid
feeling fear
The mouse is **afraid** of the cat.

af′ ter
later than; following
Darkness comes **after** daylight.
We played ball **after** school.

af ter noon' the time between noon and evening
It rained all **afternoon,** but it was clear by night.

again once more
I want to read that story **again.**

against upon or touching; on the opposite side of
The bat is **against** the wall.
His team plays **against** my team.

ahead in front
The car is **ahead** of the truck.
Jim ran **ahead** of the other boys.

air the mixture of gases around the earth
The **air** is warmer today.

air' plane a flying machine which is heavier than air and which is driven by a propeller or jet power
An **airplane** has wings.

air' port a place where airplanes can land and take off
There is an airplane at the **airport.**

all every part of; every one of
The kitten drank **all** the milk.
All dogs have ears.

al′ li ga tor   *See* **Words for Animals,** page 202.

al′ most   nearly
> I am **almost** ready.

alone   without any other person; by oneself
> Betty is walking **alone.**

along   from one end to another
> Many trees grow **along** our street.
> I walked **along** the sidewalk.

al′ so   too; in addition
> I brushed my hair. I **also** combed it.

al′ ways   at all times
> Tuesday **always** comes after Monday.

am   a form that is used with the word *I* to
                show present time
> I **am** a child.
> I **am** using a dictionary.

Amer′ i ca   the United States; North America and
Amer′ i can South America
> **America** is my country.
> I live in North **America.**
> I am an **American.**

an   any; one
> **An** elephant is **an** animal.

and   as well as; added to
                   Apples **and** oranges are fruits.
                   Three **and** two are five.

an' gry   feeling cross
                   I was **angry** because Ed hit my dog.

an' i mal   a living thing that moves about by itself
                   A dog is an **animal.**

an oth' er   one more; a different
                   May I have **another** ride?
                   Mary has gone to **another** school.

an' swer   the words you say or write when you are
                   asked a question
                   Richard gave the best **answer** to Miss
                   Cook's question.

ant   See **Words for Animals,** page 202.

an' te lope   See **Words for Animals,** page 202.
  an' te lope or **an' te lopes**

any   one out of many; some
                   You may come **any** time you wish.
                   Have you **any** money?

ap' ple   See **Words for Fruits,** page 198.

apri cot   See **Words for Fruits,** page 198.

are   a form that is used to show present
                                 time (Use with *you, we, they,* and words
                                 that mean more than one.)
                                      Are you ready? We **are** ready.
                                      Jane and Mary **are** sisters.
                                      The boys **are** swimming.

arm   the part of the body between the shoulder
                                 and the hand
                                      The little girl is raising her **arm.**

around   in a circle; on every side of; in an
                                 opposite direction
                                      The top is spinning **around.**
                                      We walked **around** the block.
                                      Please turn **around.**

as   equally; while
                                      I am **as** tall as my brother.
                                      It began to rain **as** we were eating.

ask   to try to find out by using words
                                      I will **ask** Miss Woods the answer to
                                 the question.

asleep   sleeping
                                      Joanne is **asleep.**

as par′ a gus   *See* **Words for Vegetables,** page 200.

as′ ter   *See* **Words for Flowers,** page 196.

as' tro naut   a man who travels in a spaceship
     The **astronaut** is wearing a space suit for the space flight.

at   in; on; when the time is
     Charles is **at** school.
     Tim was waiting **at** the corner.
     I eat breakfast **at** seven o'clock.

ate   *See* **eat.**

au' di ence   a group of people who hear or see
     A man is speaking to the **audience.**
     The **audience** is listening to him.

aunt   a sister of one's father or mother; the wife of one's uncle
     My mother's sister is my **aunt.**

au' thor   a person who writes books or stories
     Who is the **author** of the book?

au' tumn   the season between summer and winter; fall
     Some trees lose their leaves in the **autumn.**

awake   not asleep
     Bob is **awake,** but John is asleep.

away   from a place; at a distance
     Jerry is **away** at camp.
     Stay **away** from the river.

ba′ by
   ba′ bies

a young child
   Our **baby** is learning to crawl.

back

the upper part of the body opposite the front part; the opposite of *front*
   Tom is lying on his **back.**
   Philip sits in the **back** of the room.

bad

not good
   We played indoors because the weather was **bad.**
   Sally has a **bad** cold.

bag

a sack or container which is made of cloth, paper, leather, or plastic; a traveling case; a pocketbook
   The marbles are in a **bag.**
   Father put the **bag** in the car.
   Mrs. Roberts has a blue **bag.**

bake
   bak′ ing

to cook by dry heat, usually in an oven
   Mother will **bake** a cake in the oven.
   The cook was **baking** a pie.

ball   something that is round; a game in which a ball is used

> Here is a **ball** of string.
> Most boys like to play **ball.**

ball   a large party or dance

> Cinderella danced at the **ball.**

bal loon'   a bag which can be blown up with air

> A **balloon** is often made of thin rubber.

ba nana   *See* **Words for Fruits,** page 198.

bank   a place to keep money

> I put my money in the **bank.**

bark   the covering of a tree

> The trunk and branches of the tree are covered with **bark.**

bark   the sharp cry of a dog

> The dog's **bark** is loud.

barn   a large building for storing farm crops and keeping farm animals

> The farmer stores hay in his **barn.**

base' ball   a game played with a bat and a ball by two teams; the ball used in the game

> Many boys play **baseball.**
> The pitcher threw the **baseball.**

base′ ment   the room below the first floor of a building, sometimes below ground
There is a washing machine in the **basement.**

bas′ ket   something, often made by weaving, which is used for carrying or holding things
We filled the **basket** with apples.

bat   a stick used to hit the ball in baseball
Boys play baseball with a **bat.**

bat   See **Words for Animals,** page 202.

bath   the washing of the body
He took a **bath** in the bathtub.

be
been
be′ ing   I will **be** here at ten o'clock.
Carl and Ned have **been** to the library.
The children are **being** quiet.

bean   See **Words for Vegetables,** page 200.

bear   See **Words for Animals,** page 202.

beat
beat
beat′ en   to hit again and again; to do better than; to mix by stirring quickly
The boy **beats** the drum.
Our team **beat** Jack's team last week.
Mother has **beaten** the eggs.

beau' ti ful   very pretty to see or hear
> I picked a **beautiful** flower.

bea' ver   *See* **Words for Animals,** page 202.

be cause'   for the reason that
> Our grass is brown, **because** we have not had rain.

be come'   to come to be; to happen to
   be came'   Some seeds **become** plants.
   be come'   What **became** of the popcorn?
   be com' ing   The girl has **become** a dancer.
> The weather is **becoming** warmer.

bed   something which is used to sleep on; a piece of ground where plants are grown
> I sleep in a **bed.**
> Flowers are growing in the flower **bed.**

bee   *See* **Words for Animals,** page 202.

been   *See* **be.**

beet   *See* **Words for Vegetables,** page 200.

bee' tle   *See* **Words for Animals,** page 202.

be fore'   in front of; earlier than; earlier
> The pilot is standing **before** the class.
> **Before** school, Tim played marbles.
> I have read this book **before.**

be gin'   to start
    be gan'   When do the races **begin**?
    be gun'   It **began** to snow.
    be gin' ning   The boys have **begun** the game.
                     Leaves are **beginning** to fall.

be hind'   at the back of; late
                     Mike sits **behind** Martha.
                     Father is **behind** in his work.

be lieve'   to think something is true or real; to feel
                 sure
                     I **believe** what he says.
                     I **believe** I can do that.

bell   a hollow metal cup that rings when struck
                 by a kind of hammer
                     Did someone ring the **bell**?

be low'   lower than; beneath or under
                     The temperature is **below** zero.
                     The subway runs **below** the street.

be side'   at the side of; close to
                     The table is **beside** the chair.
                     Stand **beside** me.

be sides'   in addition to
                     Many boys **besides** Tom were late.

best   *See* **good** *and* **well.**

bet' ter   *See* **good** *and* **well.**

be tween'   in the space from one object, person, or time to another; from each of

Sue is sitting **between** Mother and Father.

He came **between** one and two o'clock.

Between us, Jim and I had a dollar.

bi' cy cle   something to ride which has two wheels, one behind the other

I rode my **bicycle** to school.

big   large

big' ger   John ate a **big** piece of cake.

big' gest   Mary's piece of cake was **bigger** than John's.

Paul had the **biggest** piece of all.

bird   *See* **Birds,** page 211.

birth' day   the day of the year on which a person was born

My **birthday** is in May.

bite   • the amount of something which is bitten off by the teeth; a cut made by the teeth

Ronnie took a **bite** of the apple.

Ruth has a dog **bite** on her hand.

• to cut into with the teeth; to sting

bit   I hope the dog doesn't **bite** me.

bit' ten   A mosquito **bit** Tommy.

bit' ing   Who has **bitten** into this chocolate?

The cold wind is **biting** my cheeks.

black' ber ry   *See* **Words for Fruits,** page 198.
black' ber ries

blan' ket   a cover for a bed, often made of wool or
                 cotton; a thick covering
                   The girl is sleeping under a warm
                 blanket.
                   A **blanket** of snow covered the earth.

blew   *See* **blow.**

block   a thick piece of something, such as wood;
                 the space between streets in a city or a
                 town
                   Joe is playing with a wooden **block.**
                   Does Timmy live in this **block**?

blood   the liquid that flows through the arteries
                 and veins in one's body
                   There is some **blood** on the boy's cut
                 finger.

blos' som   a flower, especially of a plant or a tree
                 which bears fruit
                   Here is an apple **blossom.**

blow   to make air move; to move by the force
  blew   of air
  blown   Our dog howls when the wind **blows.**
  blow' ing   Dust **blew** into my eyes.
                   The man's hat had **blown** away.
                   A gentle breeze is **blowing.**

blow   a hard hit
                 He got a bump from the hard **blow.**

blue′ ber ry   *See* **Words for Fruits,** page 198.
 blue′ ber ries

board   a thin, flat piece of wood
                 The men nailed **boards** together to
                 build a fence.

board   to get on a train, ship, or plane
                 Every day many people **board** the
                 train for the city.

boat   an object used for traveling on water
                 A red **boat** is near the shore.
                 A **boat** with a sail is in the lake.

body   the whole person or animal; the main
 bod′ ies   part
                 A cat's **body** is covered with fur.
                 The **body** of the letter tells about
                 Jim's trip.

book   sheets of paper held together at one side
                 and often printed on
                 I am reading a story in a **book.**

boot   a thick covering for the foot and part of
                 the leg
                 This **boot** is made of red rubber.

born   given birth to
                  Many babies are **born** every day.

both   the two
                  Both girls have red hair.
                  Both of them are smiling.

bot' tle   a container which is usually made of glass
                  and which has a narrow neck or opening
                  We filled the **bottle** with water.

bot' tom   the lowest part
                  A house is at the **bottom** of the hill.
                  The letter dropped to the **bottom** of
                  the mailbox.

bought   *See* **buy.**

bounce   to spring like a rubber ball
bounc' ing   The baby likes to **bounce** on his
                  father's knee.
                  The ball was **bouncing** down the stairs.

bowl   a round, deep dish
                  Mother beats eggs in a **bowl.**

bowl   to play a game in which one rolls a ball
                  down an alley at something such as a
                  wooden pin
                  Father and Bill **bowl** at the bowling
                  alley.

box
box′ es
a wooden or cardboard form to hold things
> I'll put the papers in this **box.**

boy
a male child
> The **boy** will someday be a man.

branch
branch′ es
a part of a tree, growing out from the trunk and above the ground; a part that is joined to the main part
> A bird is sitting on the **branch.**

brave
not afraid to face danger
> The fireman is **brave.**

brave
a North American Indian fighter
> The **brave** is wearing feathers.

bread
a baked food which is made with flour and other things
> Mother bought a loaf of fresh **bread** at the bakery.

break
broke
bro′ ken
break′ ing
to make something come apart; to come apart
> Should I **break** the candy in half?
> The string on the package **broke.**
> The pipe has **broken** in two places.
> Some men are **breaking** up pieces of wood for the fire.

break′ fast   the early morning meal
        We eat **breakfast** before we leave for
school.

breeze   a light wind
        The **breeze** feels cool.

brick   a block of baked clay used for building
        Brick is used to make many chimneys.

bridge   something built to carry a road over
water, railroad tracks, or another road
        The cars got to the other side of the
river by driving across the **bridge.**

bright   shining; cheerful; having a quick mind
        The sun is **bright.**
        She has a **bright** smile.
        Jane's answers show that she is a
bright child.

bring   to come with something from another
  brought   place
  bring′ ing   I will **bring** you a drink of water.
        The postman **brought** a letter.
        Harry is **bringing** a rabbit to school.

broc′ co li   *See* **Words for Vegetables,** page 200.

broke   *See* **break.**

brook   a small stream of water
         Mark caught a fish in the **brook.**

broth′ er   a boy or a man who has the same mother
and father that another person has
         Tom has one **brother** and two sisters.

brought   *See* **bring.**

brush   • a tool with hair or wires set in a handle
  brush′ es   I need a **brush** for painting.

• to use a brush
         How often do you **brush** your teeth?
         Joan **brushes** her hair every day.

brush   low bushes and trees
         The **brush** is thick in the woods.

buck′ et   a round, deep container with a handle
         The **bucket** is full of sand.

buf′ fa lo   *See* **Words for Animals,** page 203.
  buf′ fa lo or **buf′ fa loes**

bug   a crawling and sometimes flying insect
         A tiny **bug** was on the pumpkin leaf.

build   to make by putting parts together
  built   Carpenters **build** houses.
  build′ ing   Teddy **built** a fort with his blocks.
         I am **building** a toy airplane.

build′ ing   a place which has walls and a roof
        Our school is a large **building.**

bump   ● a swelling caused by hitting; a raised
       place
        The **bump** on my head hurts.
        The car shook as it went over a **bump.**

     ● to push or to hit
        Babies may **bump** into things when
       they are learning to walk.

bunch   a group of things of the same kind
   bunch′ es   This is a **bunch** of grapes.

burn   to be on fire; to set on fire
        The logs **burn** in the fireplace.
        Forest fires **burn** many trees.

bus   a large automobile for carrying many
   bus′ es or   passengers
    bus′ses   The **bus** travels across town.

bush   a plant which is smaller than a tree and
   bush′ es   which has many stems
        Blueberries grow on a **bush.**

business   work
        What is your father's **business**?

busy active; at work
> A policeman stands at the **busy** street corner.
> Mother is **busy** ironing.

but however; except
> I wanted to go, **but** I was sick.
> Everyone is here **but** Sandy.

but′ ter a food which is made from cream
> I like to put **butter** on rolls.

but′ ter fly *See* **Words for Animals,** page 203.
but′ ter flies

but′ ton a round, flat object which is used on clothing
> You fasten your coat by putting the **button** through the buttonhole.

buy to get by paying a certain price
bought > We **buy** eggs at the store.
buy′ ing > Ralph **bought** some candy for a dime.
> It is raining, and people are **buying** umbrellas.

by near; through the means of; in a measure of; no later than
> Bob lives **by** the new highway.
> Mr. Forest travels **by** airplane.
> We get milk **by** the gallon.
> **By** noon the rain had stopped.

cab′ bage	*See* **Words for Vegetables,** page 200.

cab′ in	a small, simple house usually built of wood; a room on a ship
	The **cabin** is made of logs.
	A person sleeps in a **cabin** on a ship.

cage	a place closed in by bars where birds or animals are kept
	The parrot is in a **cage.**

cake	a baked mixture of flour, eggs, sugar, and other things; a solid piece of food or other material
	Many people like chocolate **cake.**
	I bought a **cake** of soap.

calf **calves**	*See* **Words for Animals,** page 203.

call	to shout; to name
	Did you hear someone **call**?
	I **call** my cat Whiskers.

came	*See* **come.**

cam′ el   *See* **Words for Animals,** page 203.

cam′ era   a tight box for taking pictures
                   This **camera** takes good pictures.

camp   a group of tents or cabins for outdoor
                   living; a place where people live for a
                   short time
                       Tim is going to a boys′ **camp.**
                       There is a trailer **camp** outside the
                   city.

can   to be able to; may
  could   Molly **can** make good cookies.
                       I **can** play with you.
                       Ted **could** swim before I could.

can   a container made of metal
                       John opened a **can** of soup.
                       Art threw the rags in the trash **can.**

can′ dle   a stick of wax with a wick that gives off
                   light as it burns
                       The **candle** is lighted.

can′ dy   sugar and other things boiled with water
  can′ dies   and made into pieces for eating
                       Bill wants a piece of chocolate **candy.**

can′ not   not to be able to
                       I **cannot** see when my eyes are shut.

ca noe′   a light boat which is moved with paddles
             A **canoe** is a narrow boat.

can′ ta loupe *See* **Words for Fruits,** page 198.

can′ yon   a long valley with steep sides, usually with water at the bottom
             A **canyon** may be hundreds of feet deep.

cap   a small, close-fitting head cover; a cover for a bottle
             Jack will put the **cap** on his head.
             Will you take the **cap** off the bottle?

car   an automobile; an object that moves on four wheels and often carries something
             The man is driving the **car.**
             The railroad **car** is on the track.

card   a flat piece of stiff paper with many uses
             A letter is on each alphabet **card.**
             Patty made a birthday **card.**
             The directions are written on a blue **card.**

care
car′ ing   to be troubled about one's needs; to have an interest for
             Mother cats **care** for their kittens.
             Do you **care** for any dessert?
             Jill is **caring** for the children.

care′ ful   watchful
  care′ ful ly   Be **careful** when you cross the street.
               John works **carefully.**

car na′ tion *See* **Words for Flowers,** page 196.

car′ rot   *See* **Words for Vegetables,** page 200.

car′ ry   to take something from one place to
  car′ ries   another
  car′ ried   I will **carry** the suitcase.
  car′ ry ing   This train **carries** passengers.
               Father **carried** the sick boy.
               That airplane is **carrying** mail.

cas′ tle   a large building with thick walls and
              towers
               An old **castle** stood on the hill.

cat   *See* **Words for Animals,** page 203.

catch   to get hold of
  catch′ es   Let Jack **catch** the football.
  caught   One of the players **catches** the ball.
  catch′ ing   The cat **caught** a mouse last night.
               Are you **catching** any fish?

catch′ er   one who catches something in a game
               The **catcher** is a good player.

cat′ tle   cows and steers
               The **cattle** are in the barn.

caught   *See* **catch.**

cau' li flow er   *See* **Words for Vegetables,** page 200.

cave   a space underground
               It is dark inside the **cave.**

cel' ery   *See* **Words for Vegetables,** page 200.

cent   a penny; a piece of money
               Marcia paid one **cent** for a piece of
               gum.

chair   a seat for one person
               Goldilocks sat in the **chair.**

change   ● money returned to you when you have
               paid more than something cost; coins
               The grocer gave me a dime in **change.**
               Father has a pocketful of **change.**

               ● to make different; to become different;
               to go from one thing to another
chang' ing   Should I **change** my drawing?
               The weather may **change** from cloudy
               to sunny.
               Joan is **changing** her clothes.

chase   to go after to catch
chas' ing   For fun, the boys **chase** each other
               around the yard.
               Some dogs were **chasing** cars.

chat′ ter   to talk fast; to make sounds that are like
language
> Listen to the children **chatter.**
> Squirrels often **chatter** to themselves.

cheese   a food made from the thick part of milk
> May I have a piece of **cheese**?

cher′ ry   *See* **Words for Fruits,** page 198.
  cher′ ries

chick′ en   *See* **Words for Animals,** page 203.

chief   the person who leads a group
> The police **chief** is an important man.

child   a young boy or girl
  chil′ dren
> Each **child** is going to school.
> You are your parents′ **child.**
> A **child** grows every day.

chilly   cold
> The wind is **chilly** today.

chim′ ney   something to carry smoke away from a
building
> The **chimney** is on the roof.

chim pan zee′ *See* **Words for Animals,** page 203.

chip′ munk   *See* **Words for Animals,** page 203.

choc' o late   a food that is made from the seeds of a
plant and used in cooking
    Chocolate is often dark brown and
sweet.

church   a building where people worship
  church' es   My aunt was married in a **church.**

cir' cle   a closed line that is shaped like a ring;
a ring
    I drew a **circle** with my pencil.
    The children sat in a **circle.**

cir' cus   a show of clowns, acrobats, and animals
  cir' cus es   There may be dancing elephants at
the **circus.**
    The **circus** is exciting to watch.

city   a large important town where many
  cit' ies   people live
    There are many businesses in the **city.**

clam   *See* **Words for Animals,** page 203.

clean   • free from dirt
    I wash my hands to get them **clean.**

    • to take away dirt; to make neat
    We **clean** our desks before vacation.

clear
clear′ ly

easy to see through or to understand
   The air is **clear.**
   His directions were **clear.**
   He speaks **clearly.**

climb

to go up, often with the help of the hands and feet
   Jerry can **climb** the tree.
   Roses **climb** the fence in the garden.

clock

something which is used to measure and to show time
   A **clock** is not carried or worn by a person as a watch is.

close
clos′ ing

to shut
   Sam will **close** and lock the door.
   The man is **closing** the gate.

close

near; with little space between
   We live **close** to school.
   The children stood **close** together.

cloth

material made from cotton, wool, and other threads
   My jacket is made of red **cloth.**
   He cleaned the window with a **cloth.**

clothes

coverings worn on the body
   Mother hung the **clothes** on the line.
   People around the world wear many kinds of **clothes.**

cloud   a white or gray mass in the air which is
made up of tiny drops of water
There is a puffy **cloud** in the sky.

clown   a man whose job is making people laugh
The **clown** has a pie on his head.

club   • a heavy stick of wood which is thicker at
one end
The caveman used a strong **club** to
kill animals.

• a group of people with the same interest
We are starting a nature **club.**

coat   clothing to wear outdoors; a thin layer
that covers something
In winter I wear a **coat.**
Father gave the door a **coat** of paint.

cold   • a sickness which often causes a running
nose and a sore throat
Carl is sick with a **cold.**

• without heat
Ice is **cold.**

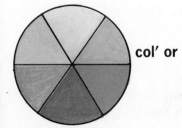

col′ or   red, yellow, blue, and the mixtures of
them
Each part of the wheel is a different
color.

come to move toward; to happen

came Will you **come** to the store with me?

come His birthday **came** on a Friday.

com′ ing Who has **come** to dinner?

The circus is **coming** to our town.

com′ pa ny friends or relatives who visit you; a
com′ pa nies business group

We have **company** at our house.

Father works for the bus **company.**

cone a shape that has a round base and that narrows to a point at the top; the seed on pine, cedar, and other evergreen trees

An ice cream **cone** has its point at the bottom.

Paul found a pine **cone** in the yard.

con′ so nant any one of the letters of the alphabet besides the vowels which are *a, e, i, o,* and *u;* a sound that stands for one of the consonant letters

The letter *b* is a **consonant.**

You can hear only one **consonant** in the word *eight.*

cook′ ie
or
cooky

a small flat cake

David ate a **cookie** which Mother had baked.

cool not warm; only somewhat cold

I wear a sweater if the air is **cool.**

corn   *See* **Words for Vegetables,** page 200.

cor′ ner   the place where two lines, sides, or

streets meet
    A ball is near the **corner** of a room.
    A **corner** of the page was torn.
    Tim Hall lives on the **corner** of the
street.

cot′ ton   a plant which has soft puffs around its
seeds; the cloth which is made from this
plant
    Some farmers raise **cotton.**
    The cloth in my dress is **cotton.**

could   *See* **can.**

count   to say the words for numbers in order; to
find out how many
    My little brother can **count** to ten.
    The teacher will **count** the children.

coun′ try   land where people do not live close to
coun′ tries one another; the land where one lives
    June lives in the city, but her uncle
lives in the **country.**
    The United States of America is our
country.

cous′ in   the child of an aunt or an uncle
    Aunt Mary's baby is my **cousin.**

cov′ er   • a part that fits over something
A blanket is a **cover** for a bed.

• to spread over
Does the snow **cover** the rooftops?

cow   *See* **Words for Animals,** page 204.

cow′ boy   a man who takes care of cattle and works
on a cattle ranch
The **cowboy** is roping the calf.

coy o′ te   *See* **Words for Animals,** page 204.

crab   *See* **Words for Animals,** page 204.

crack   • a thin break
There is a **crack** in this cup.

• to snap or to break with a quick sound
The glass may **crack** if you drop it.

crash   • a sudden, loud noise
crash′ es   What made that loud **crash**?

• to make a loud noise; to smash noisily
Thunder may **crash** during a storm.
A dropped glass often **crashes** on the
floor.

cream   the yellow, fatty part of milk
               Butter is made from **cream.**

creek   a small stream of water
               We wade in the **creek** near the farm.

crick′ et *See* **Words for Animals,** page 204.

cro′ cus   *See* **Words for Flowers,** page 196.
cro′ cus es

crop   the amount of grain, fruit, or vegetables
               grown in a season or a year
               We have a big apple **crop** this year.

cross   • a + or † shape
cross′ es   Our first-aid box has a red **cross** on
               the cover.

               • to go to the other side of
               We **cross** the street at the corner.
               The bus **crosses** the bridge.

               • not pleased; angry
               Mother was **cross** because Jackie was
               late for dinner.

crowd   a group of many people
               There was such a **crowd** at the ball
               game that there were no empty seats.

crown   a covering for the head, worn by a king or a queen

      The king wore a **crown** of gold.

cry
  cries
  cried
  cry′ ing

to shout; to make a noise from sadness or pain, usually with tears

      You should **cry** for help if you are in trouble.

      An unhappy person sometimes **cries.**
      ''Wait for me,'' Tim **cried** to the boys.
      The baby is **crying.**

cube   a solid shape with six square sides

      The block in the picture is shaped like a **cube.**

cu′ cum ber   *See* **Words for Vegetables,** page 201.

cup   a small bowl with a handle which is used for drinking

      Fill the **cup** with milk.

cut   • an opening made by something sharp

      Dan has a **cut** on his knee.

    • to remove or to open with something sharp; to shorten

cut
cut′ ting

      Mary will **cut** a picture from the newspaper with scissors.

      Yesterday I **cut** my finger with a knife.
      The man is **cutting** Sam's hair.

daf′ fo dil   *See* **Words for Flowers,** page 196.

dai′ sy   *See* **Words for Flowers,** page 196.
  dai′ sies

dance   to move the body and the feet in time to
  danc′ ing   music; to move quickly as if to music
        I like to **dance.**
        Leaves were **dancing** in the breeze.

dan′ ger ous causing trouble or harm
        Sharp knives may be **dangerous.**

dark   with little or no light; deep in color
        The house is **dark** without lights.
        Her eyes are **dark** brown.

date   *See* **Words for Fruits,** page 198.

day   the time when it is light between sunrise
       and sunset; a measure of time, about
       twenty-four hours long
        This has been a sunny **day.**
        Sunday is the first **day** of the week.

dead   without life
                  These flowers are **dead.**

dear   greatly loved
                  She is my **dear** friend.

deep   far below the top
                  Parts of the ocean are very **deep.**

deer   See **Words for Animals,** page 204.
  deer

de gree'   a point used in measuring
                  It is one **degree** below zero.

des' ert   a hot, sandy region with little water
                  Days are hot in the **desert.**

des sert'   sweets served at the end of a meal
                  We had apple pie for **dessert.**

did   See **do.**

die   to lose life
  dy' ing   If an animal doesn't eat for a long
                  time, he may **die.**
                  The rose bush is **dying.**

dif' fer ent not alike; not the same
                  A square is **different** from a circle.
                  We saw Mary three **different** times.

dig   to use hands or tools to make a hole
  dug   Our dog likes to **dig.**
  dig′ ging   He **dug** a large hole last week.
       Now he is **digging** in the garden.

dime   money worth ten cents
       Ted gave me a **dime** for ten pennies.

din′ ner   the main meal of the day, which is served at noon or in the evening
       The Greens eat **dinner** at noon.

di′ no saur   *See* **Words for Animals,** page 204.

di rec′ tion   an order or a rule for doing something; the line or way toward which a person or thing can go
       I'll read the first **direction** for making the cookies.
       A compass shows the **direction** in which you are facing.

dirt   earth or soil
  dirty   We plant seeds in **dirt.**
       My hands are **dirty.**

dish   a container for holding food
  dish′ es   Elsa will put the carrots in a **dish.**

ditch   a long, narrow place dug in the ground
  ditch′ es   Sometimes there is water in a **ditch.**
       Men dug a **ditch** along the road.

dive   to go headfirst into the water
  dived or   Nancy can **dive** well.
    dove   Al **dived** from the high diving board.
  div′ ing   Jan is **diving** into the pool.

do   to perform; to carry through on a job
  does   The dog can **do** a funny trick.
  did   Mary **does** her work well.
  done   John **did** his work this morning.
  do′ ing   I have **done** my arithmetic.
               What are you **doing**?

dog   *See* **Dogs,** page 214.

doll   a toy made to look like a person or an animal
             My **doll** looks like a little girl.

dol′ lar   a piece of money worth one hundred pennies
             Frank earned a **dollar.**

dol′ phin   *See* **Words for Animals,** page 204.

done   *See* **do.**

don′ key   *See* **Words for Animals,** page 204.

door   a part which can be moved to close an opening in a wall; the opening in a wall through which people walk
             Lock the **door** so that it will not open.
             Father had just walked in the **door.**

down   to a lower place
We walked **down** the long hill.

dream   the thoughts or pictures that are in a
person's mind when he is asleep
Ed had a funny **dream.**

dress   • a piece of clothing worn by girls and
dress' es women
Sue is wearing a red **dress** with a full
skirt.

• to put on clothes
We **dress** warmly in cold weather.
Mark **dresses** for school before he eats
breakfast.

drink   to swallow liquid
drank   I **drink** milk with every meal.
drunk   Jill **drank** two glasses of water.
drink' ing Who has **drunk** from this cup?
The boys are **drinking** lemonade.

drive   to make go
drove   **Drive** the nail into the board with the
driv' en hammer.
driv' ing Mr. Rose once **drove** a truck.
The noise has **driven** the dog away.
A man is **driving** a team of horses.

driv' er   a person who makes something, such as
a car, go
Mr. Gordon is the **driver** of the bus.

drop • a small amount of liquid, often with a round shape

    A **drop** of water is on the faucet.

• to fall; to let fall

dropped
drop′ ping
    The loose button may **drop** off your coat.

        Laura **dropped** the letter.

        The temperature is **dropping.**

drove *See* **drive.**

drum a musical instrument which makes a sound when beaten

    Use the sticks to beat the **drum.**

dry • without liquid; not wet

    The earth on the desert is **dry.**

• to remove water from; to lose water

dries
dried
dry′ ing
    I will **dry** the dishes.

    After a rainstorm the sidewalk **dries.**

    The wet shoes **dried** by the stove.

    Mother is **drying** the washing.

duck *See* **Words for Animals,** page 205.

dust
dusty
fine, dry powder in the air, often with bits of dirt in it

    There is **dust** on the table.

    Mother's hands were **dusty** after she cleaned the closet.

each every
Each child has a desk.

ear a part of the body through which one hears
I hear with both my **ears.**

ear the part of some plants on which the grain grows
This is an **ear** of corn.

ear′ ly near the beginning; before the set time
  ear′ li er We will leave **early** in the morning.
  ear′ li est I went to school **earlier** than Bob.
Which of the three buses leaves **earliest**?

earn to get in return for doing something
Do you want to **earn** a dime for cleaning the yard?

earth the planet where we live; the ground
The **earth** travels around the sun.
There are many mountains on **earth.**
We plant seeds in the soft **earth.**

east a direction; where the sun seems to rise
East is the opposite of *west.*

easy not hard to do or to get
eas′ i er This trick is **easy** to learn.
eas′ i est It is an **easier** trick than the other one.
Joe's trick is the **easiest** one of all.

eat to take food through the mouth
ate **Eat** the sandwich and drink your milk.
eat′ en The Smiths **ate** at a restaurant.
eat′ ing Jim has already **eaten** his cake.
Are you **eating** your lunch?

edge the outside part of something where it ends
Each step has a white **edge.**

egg the first form from which some animals grow; the part of a hen's egg which is used for food
Birds, turtles, and ants grow from **eggs.**
Mary Ellen will eat a fried **egg** for breakfast.

ei′ ther one or the other of the two; each of the two
You may use **either** red or blue pencils.
Flowers grow on **either** side of our yard.

elec tric' i ty   a kind of power which can be used to make light, heat, sound, and motion
　　　Years ago man learned how to use the **electricity** in nature.

el' e phant   *See* **Words for Animals,** page 205.

el' e va tor   a cage or platform which carries people or things up and down to different floors in a building
　　　Mary went to the third floor in the **elevator.**

else   other; different
　　　Will somebody **else** play with us?
　　　What **else** can we do?

emp' ty   having nothing inside
　　　Paul finished his milk, and now his glass is **empty.**

end   the last or the finish
　　　December is at the **end** of the year.

en' e my   one who is against a person or a thing
en' e mies   　　　I would rather have a friend than an **enemy.**

en' gine   a machine that gives power to make things work
　　　The **engine** in Father's car needs gasoline to work.

en gi neer'   a man who runs or makes engines; a
man who plans and builds such things
as roads and bridges
  The **engineer** waved to the children
from the train.
  The **engineer** planned a new bridge.

en joy'   to have fun with
  Most boys **enjoy** playing baseball.

enough   as much as needed
  I am hungry, because I didn't eat
enough breakfast.

en' ve lope   a paper covering in which a letter or
anything flat may be mailed
  The address and the stamp are on the
envelope.

even   flat; about the same; able to be divided
by two without a remainder
  The road was **even** instead of bumpy.
  Make the edges of the paper **even.**
  Four and six are **even** numbers.

eve' ning   the close of the day and the start of night
  We eat supper in the **evening.**

ev' er   at any time
  Have you **ever** ridden on the subway?

eve' ry   each one of a group
  Every child made a picture.

eve′ ry thing each thing; the opposite of *nothing*

Everything for lunch is on the table.

I read **everything** I can about dogs.

ex cite′ to stir up one's feelings
ex cit′ ing Parades **excite** many people.

The boys are **exciting** the dog by running around.

ex cite′ ment an excited condition

The fire at the post office caused a lot of **excitement.**

ex pect′ to plan for

The weatherman said we could **expect** rain today.

ex plain′ to give the meaning of; to tell how

Please **explain** the directions.

I hope the magician will **explain** how he does the trick.

ex plore′ to travel or to go into a place that is
ex plor′ ing almost unknown

Astronauts **explore** outer space.

The boys want to **explore** the cave.

The girls were **exploring** the old trunks in the basement.

eye a part of the body to see with; something like an eye, such as the hole in a needle

I see with both my **eyes.**

The **eye** of the needle is very small.

face

- the front part of the head where the eyes, the nose, and the mouth are; the front or most important side

    You must look in a mirror to see your own **face.**

    There are at least two hands on the **face** of a clock.

fac′ ing

- to have the front toward

    The children **face** the flag and sing.

    The houses are **facing** the street.

fair

honest; clear; not good and not bad

    Miss Smith is **fair** when she corrects papers.

    The weather is **fair** and warm.

    Since the show was only **fair,** I don't want to see it again.

fair

a place where things are shown and sometimes sold

    Mother's cake won a blue ribbon at the **fair.**

    There is a book **fair** at our school.

fairy
  fair′ ies

a make-believe person who does magical things

Peggy dressed like a **fairy** for the Halloween party.

fall
  fell
  fall′ en
  fall′ ing

to come down from above

Leaves **fall** from the maple trees.

Richard **fell** off his bicycle.

The temperature has **fallen** fifteen degrees.

Rain is **falling** now.

fall

the season between summer and winter

We rake leaves in the **fall.**

fam′ i ly
  fam′ i lies

a father, a mother, and their children

There are four boys in the Hill **family.**

far
  far′ ther
  far′ thest

a long way

John lives **far** from school.

Mike lives **farther** from school than I do.

Of all the children, Beth lives **farthest** from school.

farm

the land where one raises plants and animals

Some people drive to the country to get fresh eggs at a **farm.**

farm′ er   one who makes his living on a farm
          A good **farmer** must know how to care
          for his farm.

fast   quick; quickly
          Joe is a **fast** worker.
          I can run **fast.**

fat   • an oily mass, such as found in the bodies
          of animals and in whole milk
              The white part of uncooked bacon is
          the **fat.**

          • having a full, round body
fat′ ter   The **fat** clown is in the front.
fat′ test   He is **fatter** than the other clowns.
              The **fattest** clown makes us laugh.

fa′ ther   the male parent
          My mother and my **father** are my
          parents.

feast   a large, rich meal
          On Thanksgiving Day many people
          have a **feast.**

feath′ er   one of the parts that cover a bird's body
          The **feather** is from a bluebird.

feed   to give food to
  fed   We **feed** King dog food.
  feed′ ing   Who **fed** the baby?
          Bill is **feeding** the kittens some milk.

feel   to know through a sense of touch; to be
felt   Betty could **feel** the cold snowflakes
feel′ ing on her cheeks.
                   Do you **feel** better?
                   Jack **felt** his way along the dark hall.
                   I am **feeling** happy today.

feet   *See* **foot.**

fell   *See* **fall.**

felt   *See* **feel.**

fence   a wall, often made of wire or wood, which
                   is put around a field or a yard to keep
                   things in or out
                       The **fence** keeps the baby inside the
                   yard.

few   at least two, but not many
                       Only a **few** roses bloomed.

field   an open piece of land which usually has
                   grass or crops growing on it
                       Corn is growing in the **field.**

fight   ● a contest or a quarrel
                       The boys had a **fight.**

                   ● to hit one another; to work against
fought   Little children sometimes **fight** about
fight′ ing toys.
                       The soldiers **fought** their enemies.
                       The firemen are **fighting** the fire.

fill   to make full
             Fill the bowl with soup.
             The dentist will **fill** my tooth.

find   to look for and to get; to come upon
found   I must **find** my ticket for the show.
find' ing   Jim **found** a dime near school.
             The children are **finding** shells on the beach.

fine   thin; very good
             Rope is thick, but thread is **fine.**
             The singer had a **fine** voice.

fine   money paid by a person who has done something wrong
             Tom had to pay a **fine** at the library, because he returned his book late.

fin' ger   one of the five parts at the end of the hand
             One **finger** is raised.

fire   hot, bright flame caused by something burning
             The **fire** is spreading across the grassy field.

fire' man   one who fights a fire
fire' men   The **fireman** will fight the fire.

first   before anything or anyone else
                 January is the **first** month of the year.

fish   *See* **Words for Animals**, page 205.
  fish or **fish′ es**

flag   a piece of cloth whose colors and patterns
                 are planned to stand for a country; a piece
                 of cloth used as a signal
                 The American **flag** is red, white, and
                 blue.
                 A red **flag** on a truck means danger.

flash   a sudden light
  flash′ es   Did you see a **flash** of light?

flat   smooth and even
  flat′ ter   The top of a table is **flat.**
  flat′ test   Some land is **flatter** than other land.
                 Give me the **flattest** dish on the shelf.

flew   *See* **fly.**

float   to rest on or to be held up by a liquid or
                 by air
                 Balloons **float** in the air.

flood   a great overflow, usually of liquid
                 Because so much rain fell, there was a
                 flood.

floor	the part on which one walks in a room or in a building
	A rug is on the **floor.**

flour	a powder which is ground from grain, such as wheat, and used in baking
	Flour is used in making bread.

flow′ er	the blossom on a plant
	The **flower** on the plant is pink.

fly	to move through the air
flies	A bird can **fly** because he has wings.
flew	The airplane **flies** above the clouds.
flown	The bee **flew** into the flower.
fly′ ing	Have you **flown** in a helicopter?
	The kites are **flying** high in the sky. .

fly	See **Words for Animals,** page 205.
flies	

fog	a cloud of fine drops of water which is
fog′ gy	low in the sky
	Fog is hanging over the city.
	It is a **foggy** night.

fol′ low	to come after; to go along
	November always **follows** October.
	Follow this road up the hill.

food   anything that a plant, a person, or an
             animal eats or drinks to stay alive
                 Milk is good **food.**

foot   a part of the body on which one stands;
feet   the bottom; a measure of length
                 My **foot** is at the end of my leg.
                 The baby sat at the **foot** of the stairs.
                 A **foot** is twelve inches long.

foot′ ball   a game between two teams; the ball that
                 is used in the game
                     There are eleven players on each team
                 in **football.**
                     A player may kick, throw, or run with
                 the **football.**

for   This present is **for** you.
                 The apples are three **for** a quarter.
                 Mr. Ray works **for** a large company.

for′ est   very thick woods
                 There are many trees in a **forest.**

for get′   not to remember
for got′   If I am in a hurry, I **forget** to do things.
for got′ ten   David **forgot** to feed the goldfish.
for get′ ting   Jean has **forgotten** how to knit.
                     Dick is always **forgetting** his lunch.

fork

a handle with long points at one end which is used to pick up food
> When I eat, I use a **fork.**

fort

a strong place to protect people from the enemy
> The pioneers built a **fort** where they could be safe.

fought

See **fight.**

found

See **find.**

fox
  fox′ es or **fox**

See **Words for Animals,** page 205.

fresh

just grown or made; pure; clean
> The vegetables are **fresh.**
> The open window lets in **fresh** air.
> Mother put **fresh** sheets on the bed.

friend

a person you know well and like
> My **friend** and I like to play together.

fright′ en

to make afraid
> Did the storm **frighten** you?

frisky

lively and playful
> The **frisky** puppy is playing with the scarf.

frog

See **Words for Animals,** page 205.

from   out of; the opposite of *to;* starting with
                  Who took the flowers **from** this room?
                  I received a card **from** Al.
                  Amy comes a week **from** today.

front   first; facing forward, not to the back
                  May I sit in the **front** seat?

fruit   the part of a plant which holds the seeds
                  and which is often good to eat
                  Apples and oranges are two kinds of
                  fruit.

full   without room for any more
                  The basket is **full** of apples.

fun   a happy, gay time
                  We had **fun** playing ball.

fun' ny   causing people to laugh
  fun' ni er I will tell you a **funny** story.
  fun' ni est Some jokes are **funnier** than others.
                  Jack wore the **funniest** costume at the
                  party.

fur   the coat of hair that covers many animals
  fur' ry   The coat is made of **fur.**
                  A kitten's **fur** is soft.
                  A squirrel is a **furry** animal.

game   a kind of play

Most children know how to play the **game** hide-and-seek.

ga rage'   a building where cars and trucks are kept; a shop where cars are fixed

The car is in the **garage.**

The man at the **garage** fixed the car.

gar' den   a piece of ground where fruits, flowers, and vegetables are grown

Tomatoes are growing in this **garden.**

gas   something, such as air, which has no shape of its own and which can fill up any amount of space

The smoke from a burning candle is **gas.**

Sometimes **gas** is used in stoves.

gas' o line   a liquid which is used to make some engines run

Father buys **gasoline** for our car.

gate   a door that opens and closes in a wall or a fence

Penny closed the **gate** to keep the dog out of the garden.

gave   *See* **give.**

gen' tle   kind; soft
  gen' tly   Mother gave the baby a **gentle** pat.
               A **gentle** breeze lightly blew the leaves.
               She speaks **gently.**

ge ra' ni um   *See* **Words for Flowers,** page 196.

get   to receive or to take; to come; to become
  got   I **get** books at the library.
  got' ten   Who **got** here first?
   or got   The kittens have **gotten** bigger.
  get' ting   Barbara is **getting** a new coat.

ghost   a bodiless being, sometimes thought to be a person who has died

The story about the **ghost** scared me.

gi' ant   a huge man

In the story the **giant** held the boy inside his large hand.

gi raffe'   *See* **Words for Animals,** page 205.

girl   a female child

That **girl** is my sister.

give   to let someone or something have
  gave   I will **give** you a penny.
  giv′ en   The man **gave** the fence a coat of
  giv′ ing   paint.
          The teacher has **given** us new pencils.
          Ted is **giving** the dog a bath.

glad   pleased
          The children are **glad** that Paul is not
          sick anymore.

glass   something hard which can usually be
  glass′ es   seen through and which can be easily
          broken; a drinking cup, usually made of
          glass
          A window has a large sheet of **glass**
          set in it.
          I drink milk from a **glass.**

glove   a covering for the hand which usually has
          a place for each finger
          In chilly weather wool **gloves** keep
          your hands warm.

go   to move along
  goes   Jim will **go** to school soon.
  went   The bus **goes** past our house.
  gone   Nancy **went** to the store.
  go′ ing   The Kanes have **gone** to the beach.
          Are you **going** to the library?

goat   *See* **Words for Animals,** page 205.

gold   a bright yellow metal
                 Many rings are made of **gold.**

good   pleasing or enjoyable; well-behaved
  bet′ ter   That was a **good** show.
  best   John is a **good** boy.
                 I think plums are **better** than pears.
                 Tom is my **best** friend.

good-by′   something said when a person leaves
   or   **"Good-by,"** called the girls as they
good-bye′   left the party.

goose   *See* **Words for Animals,** page 205.
  geese

go ril′ la   *See* **Words for Animals,** page 206.

got   *See* **get.**

grade   one class in school; a mark received for
                 work done
                    Ted is in the third **grade.**
                    Beth got a high **grade** in spelling.

grand′ fa ther   the father of one's father or mother
                     My **grandfather** is the oldest
             person in our family.

grand′ moth er the mother of one's father or mother
I have two **grandmothers.**

grape *See* **Words for Fruits,** page 198.

grape′ fruit *See* **Words for Fruits,** page 198.

grass a plant with thin green shoots, or leaves, which grows on lawns, meadows, and fields
Mr. Jackson cuts the **grass** in the school yard.

grass′ hop per *See* **Words for Animals,** page 206.

great big; important
A **great** number of people watched the ball game.
George Washington was a **great** man.

grew *See* **grow.**

gro′ cer a person who sells food and some things for the home
Mother buys food every week from the **grocer.**

gro′ cery the store where food and some things for the home are sold
People shop at the **grocery.**

ground   the soil; the land
        We plant seeds in the **ground.**

group   a number of people or things together
        A **group** of boys played baseball.

grow   to become larger
  grew   As I **grow** bigger, my clothes seem
  grown   to be smaller.
  grow' ing   Tom **grew** one inch last year.
        The plant has **grown** quickly.
        Our city is **growing** fast.

growl   a deep, usually angry, sound
        Biff gave a low **growl** at the strange
    man.

gruff   being rough in actions, looks, or speech
  gruff' ly   The angry man has a **gruff** voice.
        He speaks **gruffly.**

guess   to try to give an answer when one is not
  guess' es sure
        Can you **guess** how the story ends?
        Jack often **guesses** the answers to
    riddles.

gun   a weapon which can be made to shoot
    something, such as bullets
        The cowboy put his **gun** in its holster.

had   *See* **have.**

hail   chunks of frozen rain
    During the storm, **hail** beat noisily against the window.

hair   the fine pieces growing from the skin of people and some animals
    I like to brush my **hair.**

half
halves   one of two equal parts which together make the whole of something
    Ben cut the cupcake in **half.**
    We will go in **half** an hour.

hall   a small room or narrow way in a house or building; a large room or building
    Mary's classroom is at the end of the **hall.**
    Aunt June came in the front door and left her coat in the **hall.**
    The fair was held in a large **hall.**

ham′ burg er   ground beef which is often shaped into flat patties before it is cooked
I put my **hamburger** into a bun.

ham′ mer   a tool with a handle and a head which is used to drive nails
A builder uses a **hammer.**

ham′ ster   *See* **Words for Animals,** page 206.

hand   the end part of one's arm; a pointer, such as on a clock
I have five fingers on each **hand.**
There are **hands** on a clock.

hand′ ker chief   a soft, often square, piece of cloth which is usually used to wipe the nose and the face
I use a cotton **handkerchief.**

han′ dle   • a part of a thing to be held by the hand
You carry a pail by its **handle.**

• to touch or to hold with the hand
han′ dling   **Handle** a sharp knife with care.
The nurse is **handling** the baby gently.

handy   useful
A pencil is a **handy** tool.

hang   to fasten or to be fastened to a rod, a
hung   hook, or something above
hang′ ing   Dick will **hang** up his clothes.
                  Tim **hung** the picture on the wall.
                  Clothes are **hanging** on the line.

hap′ pen   to take place
                  Many things **happen** each day.

hap′ pi ness the feeling of gladness; joy
                  We wished Nancy **happiness** on her
                  birthday.

hap′ py   glad or pleasant
  hap′ pi er   Danny is a **happy** boy.
  hap′ pi est   I feel **happier** than I did.
                  This is the **happiest** birthday I have
                  ever had.

hard   firm; not soft; not easy
                  The candy was so **hard** that I could
                  not break it in half.
                  Jim had a **hard** time carrying the heavy
                  box.

hard′ ly   not quite; just about
                  We **hardly** had time to catch the bus.

hat   a covering for the top part of the head
                  You wear a **hat** on your head.

hatch	to come out of an egg
hatch' es	I saw a chick **hatch** from its shell.
	A baby duck **hatches** in about a month.

have	to own; to be forced; to hold
has	I **have** a new ring.
had	Tom **has** to go to bed early.
hav' ing	Our class **had** a puppet show last week.
	Dick is **having** a birthday soon.

hay   grasses or plants, such as clover, which are cut and dried and used as food for some animals

Horses, cows, and sheep eat **hay.**

he
his
him
the boy, man, or male animal spoken about

He is my uncle.

His name is Mr. Baker.

I helped **him** clean the basement.

The truck in the driveway is **his.**

head   the top part of the body; the front; the top

The man has hair on his **head.**

Larry marched at the **head** of the parade.

The **head** of a nail is at one end, and the point is at the other.

hear
heard
hear' ing

to receive sounds through the ear; to learn by listening
>Can you **hear** Jim whispering?
>We **heard** the good news.
>Tim was **hearing** noises in the dark.

heart

the part of the body inside the chest that pumps the blood and helps to keep the body alive; a ♡ shape
>When you run, your **heart** beats faster.
>The valentine **heart** is red.

heat

the opposite of *cold*
>The sun gives off **heat.**

heavy
heav' i er
heav' i est

hard to lift because of weight
>The **heavy** suitcase was hard to carry.
>This box is **heavier** than yours.
>Father carried the **heaviest** box.

held

See **hold.**

hel' i cop' ter

an aircraft without wings which is lifted and moved by whirling blades on top and often at the back
>A **helicopter** is able to fly straight up when it leaves the ground.

hel lo'

a greeting you say when you first see or talk to someone
>**"Hello!"** said Ann when she met Jill.

help   to be useful to; to do something for
        May I **help** you?
        My eyeglasses **help** me to see.

her   the girl, woman, or female animal spoken
hers   about; belonging to her; a form of *she*
        Cathy is my friend, and I like **her.**
        She left **her** doll in the yard.
        The doll bed is **hers,** too.

herd   a number of the same kind of animal,
such as cows, that are together
        Cowboys watched the **herd** of cattle.

here   in this place; to this place
        "Put the book **here,** not there," said
the teacher.
        Here they come!

hi bis′ cus   *See* **Words for Flowers,** page 196.

hide   to keep out of sight; to put away
hid   You **hide,** and we will try to find you.
hid′ den   Mother **hid** the presents.
  or **hid**   Where have you **hidden** the candy?
hid′ ing   The boys are **hiding** from Allan.

high   tall; above the ground
        The top of the bookcase is too **high**
for me to reach.
        Jets fly **high** in the sky.

hill   a raised part of the earth which is smaller than a mountain

The children like to climb to the top of the **hill.**

him   the boy, man, or male animal spoken about; a form of *he*

I had a race with Ed, and I beat **him.**

hip po pot' a mus   *See* **Words for Animals,** page 206.

his
  his   belonging to him; a form of *he*

Jerry is looking for **his** jacket.
The red jacket is **his.**

hit
  hit   to come against with force
  hit' ting   The low branch may **hit** your head.
Paul **hit** the ball with a bat.
The boy is **hitting** his brother.

hold
  held   to take and keep; not to let go
  hold' ing   Jack will **hold** the package.
Susie **held** the kitten in her lap.
Who is **holding** the flag?

hole   an open or hollow place
The puppy dug a **hole** in the garden.
There is a **hole** in my pocket.

hol' low   empty
A chipmunk ran into the **hollow** log.

home a place where one lives
In the morning I leave **home** and go to school.

hon' ey a sweet, yellow liquid made by bees from the liquid of flowers
Honey is sweet and sticky.

honk to make a sound like the cry of a wild goose
Car horns can **honk** loudly.

hook a curved piece of metal or wood for catching or holding something
There is a **hook** in the closet.
Jack put a worm on the **hook.**

hope to wish
hop' ing I **hope** you will play with me.
Many boys **hope** to become famous astronauts.
Mother is **hoping** Susan will come today.

horn a hard growth on the heads of some animals, such as cattle; something hollow which is blown through to make a sound; a warning signal, as on a car
A goat has **horns.**
Tom tooted the **horn** in time to the music.
Father honked the **horn** at the dog.

hor′ net   *See* **Words for Animals,** page 206.

horse   *See* **Words for Animals,** page 206.

hos′ pi tal   a place where sick or hurt people or
                     animals are taken care of
                         Doctors and nurses work at the
                     hospital.

hot   having much heat; having a burning
hot′ ter   feeling
hot′ test   A fire is **hot.**
                         The sun will make the air **hotter.**
                         This is the **hottest** day we have had.

hour   a measure of time
                         There are sixty minutes in an **hour.**

house   a building where people live
                         A family lives in the **house.**
                         The **house** has six rooms.

how   in what way; to what degree
                         I don't know **how** to do that.
                         How tall is your brother?

howl   to give a long, loud, and often sad cry
                         Our dog can **howl** like a wolf.
                         Did you hear the wind **howl** during the
                     storm?

hun' dred   ten times ten; the number for which 100
                    stands
                        Ninety-nine and one make a **hundred.**
                        One **hundred** pennies equal a dollar.

hung   *See* **hang.**

hun' gry   feeling the need for food
                        I am always **hungry** before dinner.

hunt   to look for or to chase
                        We will **hunt** for peanuts at my party.
                        Uncle Joe likes to **hunt** deer.

hur' ri cane   a storm with strong, whirling winds and
                    heavy rain
                        The **hurricane** swept along the coast.

hur' ry   to move quickly
hur' ries   Some people **hurry** to catch the train.
hur' ried   Sue **hurries** to meet her friends.
hur' ry ing   I slept late, so I **hurried** to school.
                        Mr. Johnson is **hurrying** to work.

hurt   to cause pain to
hurt   You can **hurt** yourself with a knife.
                        Tom **hurt** his knee when he fell.

hus' band   a married man; a man who has a wife
                        My father is my mother's **husband.**

I	the one who is speaking or writing
me	Mark and **I** play together.
my	He asked **me** to play ball.
mine	That is **my** baseball.
	The bat is **mine,** too.

ice	water that has been frozen
icy	When water freezes, it becomes **ice.**
	In winter some roads are **icy.**

ice cream	a dessert made by mixing and freezing cream, sugar, eggs, and flavoring
	Sam likes strawberry **ice cream.**

idea	a plan or a thought
	Sally has a good **idea** for a story.

if	in case; whether
	If it snows, we will not go.
	I wonder **if** they will come.

im por' tant	chief; of value
	New York is an **important** city.
	It is **important** to follow the rules.

in   inside; within; the opposite of *out*
                          Mr. Jones is **in** the bank.
                          They live **in** Michigan.
                          I can be there **in** an hour.

inch   a measure of length
  inch′ es   The line is an **inch** long.
                          An **inch** is smaller than a foot.

In′ di an   a member of the native American race; a
                         person from India
                          The **Indian** is weaving a blanket.
                          People in India are called **Indians.**

In′ di an   Paint′ brush
                         See **Words for Flowers,** page 196.

in′ sect   a small animal which has three parts to
                         its body, six legs, and sometimes wings
                          A fly is an **insect.**

in′ side   the part within; the opposite of *outside*
                          The **inside** of the house is dark.

in′ to   to the inside of; to a certain condition
                          He is going **into** the house.
                          We ran **into** rain on our way home.

iris   *See* **Words for Flowers,** page 196.
  iris es

iron   ● a useful metal from which things, such as machines and tools, are made; a tool with a handle and a wide, flat bottom
>   A fire hydrant is made of **iron.**
>   Our **iron** uses electricity.

● to take the wrinkles from clothes by using a heated iron
>   Mother **irons** our clothes.

is   a form that is used to show present time (Use with words that mean only one, except the words *I* and *you*.)
>   It **is** nine o'clock.
>   Tom **is** glad that he **is** in the play.
>   The baby **is** crying.

is′ land   a piece of land that has water on all sides
>   We had to take a boat to the **island.**

it   the thing, the animal, or the person spoken about
>   Take the dish, and handle **it** carefully.
>   The dog chased the squirrel, but he could not catch **it.**

its   belonging to the thing or the animal spoken about
>   I saw a jet and heard **its** roar.
>   The dog hurt **its** paw.

jack′ et   a short coat
         The boy is wearing a green **jacket.**

jar   a wide-mouthed container, usually made
         of glass, for holding liquids or solids
         The **jar** was filled with applesauce.

jet   a stream of liquid or gas sent with force
         A **jet** of water came from the fountain.

jet plane   an airplane with an engine which forces
         out a stream of hot air and gas powerful
         enough to fly the airplane
         A **jet plane** can fly very fast.

job   work; work for pay
         Washing windows is a hard **job.**
         George has a **job** as a paper boy.

join   to put together; to become a part of
         We **join** hands to make a circle.
         My older brother may **join** a club
         at school.

joke　　　　something said or done which usually makes people laugh
　　　　　　　John told a funny **joke.**

jol' ly　　　full of cheer
　jol' li er　　The man is **jolly.**
　jol' li est　　He is **jollier** than his wife.
　　　　　　　He is the **jolliest** person I know.

joy　　　　much happiness
　　　　　　　Thanksgiving is a time of **joy.**

juice　　　the liquid part that comes from fruits,
　juicy　　　vegetables, and meat
　　　　　　　I like to drink orange **juice.**
　　　　　　　Some tomatoes are **juicy.**

jump　　　to leap into the air
　　　　　　　Sam can **jump** higher than the other boys in his class.

jun' gle　　land covered with a thick growth of trees and bushes, especially in the tropics
　　　　　　　There are often tigers in the **jungle.**

just　　　　exactly; a short time ago; only
　　　　　　　I have **just** one penny.
　　　　　　　They have **just** left.
　　　　　　　The noise is **just** the door rattling.

kan ga roo'   *See* **Words for Animals,** page 206.

keep
  kept
  keep' ing

to have without giving away; to have and to take care of
May I **keep** the red pencil?
Robert **kept** the dime he found.
Chuck is **keeping** Fred's dog for him.

key

a small piece of metal for opening and closing a lock; one of many parts used for playing a piano or working a typewriter
Mary turned the **key** in the lock.
You must push down a typewriter **key.**

kick

to strike with the foot or feet
He can **kick** the football.
You **kick** the water when you swim.

kind

being good to others; gentle
Our teacher is **kind** to us.

kind

type; sort
What **kind** of ice cream do you like?

king   a man who rules a country
Sometimes a **king** wears a crown.

kitch' en   a room where food is made ready
The stove and the sink are in the
kitchen.

kite   a light wooden frame covered with cloth
or paper and flown in the air at the end of
a string
John put a long tail on his **kite.**

kit' ten   See **Words for Animals,** page 206.

knew   See **know.**

knife   a tool that has a handle and a sharp edge
knives   We cut meat with a **knife.**

knock   to hit hard; to bump into and make fall
I will **knock** on the door.
Did you **knock** the lamp over?

know   to be sure; to be familiar with
knew   You **know** how to spell many words.
known   He **knew** Mary before he met Joan.
know' ing   Alice has **known** that song for years.
Keep him from **knowing** the secret.

kum' quat   See **Words for Fruits,** page 199.

lad   a boy
The **lad** grew to be a strong man.

lad′ der   a set of steps which are fastened into two long pieces of wood or metal and which can usually be moved from place to place
The man used a **ladder** to reach the roof.

la′ dy   a woman
la′ dies   Miss Brooks is a young **lady.**

la′ dy bug   *See* **Words for Animals,** page 206.

lake   a body of water surrounded by land
We sailed in a boat around the **lake.**
A **lake** is often larger than a pond.

lamb   *See* **Words for Animals,** page 207.

lame   having a hurt leg; not able to walk well
The **lame** dog has a sore paw.
Jack was **lame** after he fell.

land   ●the hard part of the earth's surface; ground; a country

Earth is covered with **land** and water.

Most cities have **land** set aside for parks.

America is our **land.**

●to bring down to earth

Pilots **land** the planes on a runway.

large   very big; great

An elephant is very **large.**

last   after all the rest

The little boy is the **last** person in line.

I ate the **last** plum.

last   to continue; to go on

The show will **last** an hour.

We must water the flowers so that they will **last** longer.

late   after the usual time; the opposite of *early*

Hurry, or you will be **late** for dinner.

late' ly   not long ago; a little while ago

Have you read a book **lately**?

Lately we added to our library.

laugh   to make happy sounds to show that you have seen or heard something funny

People **laugh** at funny stories.

lay   to put down; to put in place
  laid   Jill will **lay** the book on the table.
  lay′ ing   Ellen **laid** the blanket on the bed.
              The workman is **laying** the bricks.

la′ zy   not very willing to work
  la′ zi er   Alice was too **lazy** to clean her room.
  la′ zi est   Herb is **lazier** than his brother.
              Sally is the **laziest** girl I know.

lead   to go first, often to show the way
  led   The boy **leads** the pony.
  lead′ ing   A pretty girl **led** the parade.
              Jack was **leading** in the race.

lead′ er   one who shows the way or leads
              Mr. Long is the **leader** of the band.

leaf   a thin, flat, and usually green part that
  leaves   grows on plants and trees
              A **leaf** blew down from the tree.

learn   to find out; to come to know
              Children **learn** many things in school.
              We will **learn** that poem.

leath′ er   the skin of certain animals that has been
              tanned, or treated in a special way
              An alligator's skin is often used to
              make **leather.**

leave
  left
  leav′ ing
	to go away; to let stay behind; to let stay a certain way
	    Henry will **leave** on the early bus.
	    Jack **left** his coat at school.
	    Betty is **leaving** the door open.

left   a direction; the opposite of *right*
                        The boy is raising his **left** arm.
                        The bus made a **left** turn.

leg   a part of the body on which people and animals stand or walk; anything used like a leg
                        A person has two **legs.**
                        Most tables have four **legs.**

lem′ on   *See* **Words for Fruits,** page 199.

lem on ade′ a drink made from the juice of lemons, sugar, and water
                        Lemonade with ice tastes good.

leop′ ard   *See* **Words for Animals,** page 207.

less   smaller in amount; not so much
                        Pat spent **less** than a dollar.

let
  let
  let′ ting
	to allow
	    I will **let** you ride my bicycle.
	    Last week Jan **let** Beth use her pen.
	    Father is **letting** Sport ride in the car.

let′ ter   one of the written or printed signs or marks which are used to stand for sounds in words; a written message

The last **letter** in our alphabet is *z*.
He mailed the **letter.**

let′ tuce   *See* **Words for Vegetables,** page 201.

li′ brary   a place where books are kept; a large
li′ brar ies   group of books

Mary got her book at the **library.**
We have books about space in our classroom **library.**

lie   an untrue statement or story which is told to cheat or mislead

It is not right to tell a **lie.**

lie   to have the body out flat; to be flat
lay   Ron likes to **lie** on the beach.
lain   The bike **lay** on the ground.
ly′ ing   Mother has **lain** on the bed for a nap.
The sign is **lying** on its side.

life   the condition of being alive; the time in
lives   which people, animals, and plants are alive

A stone has no **life.**
Grandfather has lived here all his **life.**

lift   to raise or to pick up
                  You should **lift** a baby carefully.

light   easy to lift; the opposite of *heavy;* gentle;
                  pale
                      This box is **light.**
                      There was a **light** tap on the door.
                      On clear days the sky is **light** blue.

light   what helps us to see; brightness
                      You should have good **light** when you
                  read.
                      The sun gives us **light.**

like   almost the same as
                      The rumble of the heavy truck
                  sounded **like** thunder.

like   to be pleased with; to enjoy
                      Do you think Jim will **like** our present?

line   a long rope or string; a row; a long mark
                      Mother hung a towel on the **line.**
                      The children are standing in **line.**
                      John wrote his name on the top **line.**

line   to put paper or cloth along the inside of
lin' ing   something, such as a box or a coat
                      The girls will **line** the box with paper.
                      Mother is **lining** my coat.

li′ on   *See* **Words for Animals,** page 207.

liq′ uid   something, such as water, that flows
                    easily; not a solid or a gas
                    Milk is a **liquid.**

lis′ ten   to try to hear; to pay attention to by
                    hearing
                    I often **listen** to the radio.

lit′ tle   small; not big; not much
                    My **little** sister is learning to read.
                    I poured a **little** water on the plant.

live   to be alive; to make your home
  liv′ ing   You may **live** to be ninety years old.
                    On which street do you **live**?
                    The Smiths are now **living** in Texas.

live′ ly   full of life; frisky
                    The **lively** dogs chased one another.

liz′ ard   *See* **Words for Animals,** page 207.

load   • the things being carried
                    The truck carries a **load** of lumber.

                    • to put in something to be carried
                    The men will **load** the moving van.

lob′ ster   *See* **Words for Animals,** page 207.

lock   to fasten something, such as a door, so that it will not open

You can **lock** the door with the key.

Father **locks** the trunk of the car.

log   a piece of wood as it comes from a tree

I'll put another **log** in the fireplace.

long   taking much time; having a great measure from one end to another; the opposite of *short*

Miss Lane read to us for a **long** time.

Ted found a **long** rope.

look   to try to see; to pay attention to by seeing

Look both ways before you cross the street.

You should **look** at the person who is giving a report in class.

loose   not tied; not tight enough

Jill tied the dog to the fence, but he got **loose.**

My shoes are too **loose.**

lose
lost
los' ing   not to be able to find; to have missing; not to win

If you don't keep your ticket in a safe place, you may **lose** it.

My little brother **lost** his first tooth.

The girls are **losing** the race.

lot
a piece of land or ground; a great number
We play ball in the empty **lot.**
There are a **lot** of books in the library.

loud
loud' ly
having a great sound; not quiet; very noisy
Thunder makes a **loud** sound.
The boys called **loudly.**

iove
to have a close feeling for
I **love** my parents.

love' ly
beautiful; very pleasing
The golden sunset was **lovely.**

low
near the ground or the bottom; not high
The girl put her doll on a **low** chair.
Tim has a **low** voice.

low' er
to let down
We **lower** the window shades at night.

luck
something good or bad which seems to happen by chance
They had good **luck** fishing.
I had bad **luck** when I broke my leg.

lunch
lunch' es
a light meal, usually eaten in the middle of the day
Many children eat **lunch** at school.

ma chine′ a thing made up of parts for doing work
  Mother sews faster on a sewing **machine** than she does by hand.

made *See* **make.**

mag′ ic something supposedly done by a secret charm
  In the story the witch used **magic** to turn the prince into a frog.

ma gi′ cian one who does tricks, as if by magic
  The **magician** can do many tricks.

maid a woman helper; a young girl
  Mrs. Palmer has a **maid** to help her.
  In a poem a girl is sometimes called a **maid.**

mail letters, packages, magazines, and other things sent through the post office
  The **mail** was left in the mailbox.

make   to build; to put together; to cause to be
  made   The boys will **make** a tree hut.
  mak′ ing   Mrs. Smith **made** a good chocolate
              cake.
                  The sun is **making** the sidewalk hot.

man   a grown-up boy
  men   My father is a **man.**

many   a great number of
                  There are **many** feet in a mile.

mar′ ble   a kind of hard rock which takes a beautiful
              polish; a small hard ball used in games
                  Some buildings are made of **marble.**
                  Sam has a red **marble.**

march   to walk like a soldier by keeping in step
  march′ es   with others
                  The boys will **march** in the parade.
                  Jack **marches** with the band.

mar′ i gold   *See* **Words for Flowers,** page 197.

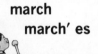

mark   a line or a dot; a sign; a grade
                  Ellen made a **mark** with her crayon.
                  A period is a punctuation **mark.**
                  Janet received a good **mark** on her
              paper.

mar′ ket   a place where things are bought and sold
Ellen bought some apples and pears at the **market.**

mat′ ter   the trouble
What is the **matter** with the boy who is crying?

may
might
to be allowed; to be possible
May I have a cookie?
If we don't hurry, we **may** be late.
Mother told me I **might** go.

may′ be   possibly; perhaps
Maybe it will rain.

me   the person speaking; a form of *I*
Bill gave Tom and **me** some candy.

mead′ ow   a grassy field
The grass in the **meadow** will be cut and dried for hay.

meal   food which is prepared and eaten
The evening **meal** is on the table.

meal   grain which has been ground
Some corn is ground into **meal.**

mean
meant
mean' ing

to have as its thought; to have in mind
I don't know what the words **mean.**
Tom didn't know what the teacher **meant.**
Ann has been **meaning** to write you.

mean

unkind
It is **mean** to make fun of someone.

meas' ure

an amount or a size
An inch is a **measure** of length.

meat

the flesh of animals which is used for food
We buy **meat** at the store.
Mother cooked the **meat** for dinner.

meet
met
meet' ing

to join; to get together; to be introduced to
The children **meet** each other on the way to school.
The boys **met** on the playground.
Joanne's mother is **meeting** the new teacher.

meet' ing

a group of people who come together for some reason
Mother has gone to a **meeting** of parents and teachers.
The science club had a **meeting.**

men

See **man.**

mer′ ry   full of fun; gay
  mer′ ri er   What a **merry** time we had!
  mer′ ri est   This was a **merrier** party than the last one.
    Everyone had the **merriest** time at the circus.

mes′ sage   information sent from one person to another
    Ann took a **message** for her father over the telephone.
    We sent a telegraph **message.**

met   *See* **meet.**

mice   *See* **mouse.**

mid′ dle   a point halfway between the ends or the sides
    The white line is in the **middle** of the road.

might   *See* **may.**

might   strength; great power
  mighty   Beth swam with all her **might.**
    The giant was a **mighty** man.

mile   a measure of distance
    A **mile** is many times longer than a foot or a yard.

milk   a white liquid which comes from cows and some other mother animals and which is used as food
       Milk is a food which helps to make you healthy.

mind   the part of a person which thinks, feels, chooses, and decides
       Terry has a good **mind.**

min' ute   a measure of time; a short time
       There are sixty seconds in a **minute** and sixty minutes in an hour.
       I'll be ready in a **minute.**

miss   not to catch, to hit, or to get; to feel sad
miss' es   when away from someone or something
       You may **miss** the bus if you sleep late.
       Did the catcher **miss** the ball?
       Grandmother **misses** the children after she leaves them.

Miss   a title given to a girl or a woman who is not married
       Miss Smith is getting married.

mit' ten   a covering for the hand which has one place for the thumb and another place for the other fingers
       The **mitten** is made of wool yarn.

mon' ey   coins and paper bills which are used to pay for things
    The United States government makes the **money** which we use.

mon' key   *See* **Words for Animals**, page 207.

month   one of the twelve periods of time which together make a year
    December is the last **month** of the year.

moon   a body in the sky that moves around the earth about once a month
    There is a full **moon** tonight.

more   greater in number; additional
    Three books are **more** than two books.
    Do you want **more** potatoes?

morn' ing   the first part of the day; the time between midnight and noon
    Morning comes before afternoon.

mos qui' to   *See* **Words for Animals**, page 207.
  mos qui' toes

most   greatest number of; almost all
    William was the winner because he had the **most** votes.
    Most people like to read.

moth' er   the female parent
                   A **mother** takes care of her children.
                   I help **Mother** by watching the baby.

mo' tor   the part that makes a machine go; an
                   engine
                   A car has a **motor.**

moun' tain   a very high hill
                   A **mountain** may have snow at its top
                   all year round.

mouse   See **Words for Animals,** page 207.
mice

mouth   the opening in the face for taking in food;
                   an opening
                   When you talk, you must open and
                   close your **mouth.**
                   Bushes hid the **mouth** of the cave.

move   to change from one position or place to
mov' ing   another
                   The men must **move** the furniture.
                   I can **move** each finger on my hand.
                   Our neighbors are **moving** to a
                   different city.

Mr.   a title for a man; the abbreviation for the
                   word *Mister*
                   Mr. Jones is Kathy's father.

Mrs.　　a title for a woman who is married; an abbreviation for the word *Mistress*
　　　　Mrs. Hall is Mr. Hall's wife.

much　　a great amount of; greatly
　　　　There was **much** excitement at the Halloween party.
　　　　I am **much** taller than I was last year.

mud　　earth which is wet and sticky
　mud′ dy　　The little girl played in the **mud.**
　　　　Her shoes are **muddy.**

mu′ sic　　the art of putting sounds together in some kind of order
　　　　Music can be sung or played on an instrument.

mu si′ cian　　a person who sings or plays a musical instrument with great skill
　　　　The man who played the piano is a fine **musician.**

must　　have to
　　　　We **must** go now, or we will be late.
　　　　All people **must** have water to drink.

my　　belonging to me; a form of *I*
　mine　　**My** book is on the table.
　　　　The book on the table is **mine.**

nail

a thin piece of metal, pointed at one end and flat at the other; the hard covering at the end of a finger or a toe

The carpenter used a hammer to drive the **nail** into the wood.

I cut the **nail** on my thumb.

name

the special word or words used to stand for a person, an animal, or a thing; a title

When a baby is born, he is given a **name** by his parents.

My friend's **name** is Mary Ann Brown.

What is the **name** of the game you are playing?

near
near' ly

not far from; close to

They live **near** Los Angeles but far from Boston.

It is **nearly** time for bed.

neck

the part of the body between the head and the shoulders

A necklace is around the girl's **neck.**

A giraffe has a long **neck.**

need   must have; should have
                            People **need** food to live.
                            You **need** a coat in cold weather.

neigh′ bor   a person who lives in the next house or in
                            a nearby house
                            We share a garage with our **neighbor.**

nest   a place built by birds for their eggs; a
                            place built by some animals and insects
                            A bird often uses string, twigs, and
                            grass to build his **nest.**
                            Wasps built a **nest** under the roof.

nev′ er   at no time
                            You should **never** play with matches.

new   not used; not known before
                            That shiny bicycle is **new.**
                            I have a **new** friend.

news   story of something that has just happened
                            Mike told us the **news** about the fire.
                            Father watches the **news** on television.

news′ pa per   printed sheets of paper which report
                            the happenings of the day and other
                            things of interest to people
                            The **newspaper** has reports of what is
                            happening around the world.

next   nearest; following at once
            Frank is sitting **next** to the window.
            What can we do **next**?

nice   pleasing
  nice′ ly   Joan is a **nice** person.
            She sings **nicely.**

nick′ el   a piece of money equal to five cents
            You can buy a candy bar for a **nickel.**

night   the time between evening and morning
            I like to watch the moon and the stars
        at **night.**

no   the opposite of *yes;* not any
            No, *i* is not before *a* in *rain.*
            A snake has **no** legs.

noise   a sound, usually not pleasant
  nois′ i ly   The gun made a loud **noise.**
  noisy   Some children shouted **noisily.**
            The old car's engine is **noisy.**

noon   the middle of the day
            We eat lunch at **noon.**

north   a direction
            North is the opposite of *south.*
            Canada is **north** of the United States.

nose   a part of the face above the mouth
A person breathes and smells with his **nose.**

not   a word which is like *no*
The land is dry, because we have **not** had rain.
There is **not** an *e* in the word *saw.*

note   a short written message; a sign in music to stand for a sound
Mother wrote a **note** to tell us where she was going.
I try not to miss a **note** when I play the piano.

noth′ ing   not a thing
The box is empty, because there is **nothing** in it.

now   at this time
Do your work **now,** not later.

num′ ber   a word or a sign that tells how many; a certain amount of
Two is a **number.**
A **number** of boys went swimming.

nut   a dry fruit or seed with a hard shell
Many kinds of **nuts** are good to eat.
The squirrel nibbled at a **nut.**

ocean
the body of salt water that covers a great part of the earth; one of the large parts of this main body of water
Ships travel across the **ocean**.
The Atlantic **Ocean** is east of the United States.

o'clock
an abbreviation for *of the clock*
It is nine **o'clock**.

oc′ to pus
oc′ to pus es
See **Words for Animals,** page 207.

of
belonging to; made from; from; that is
Sandy cleared the top **of** the desk.
The girl held a bunch **of** flowers.
Do you want a piece **of** the pie?
I live in the state **of** Vermont.

off
away from; not on
The wind blew the man's hat **off** his head.
The water has been turned **off**.

of′ ten   many times
>In the summer we **often** go to the beach.

oh   a word to express surprise, joy, or other strong feelings
>**Oh,** I broke my glasses!

okra   *See* **Words for Vegetables,** page 201.

old   the opposite of *young;* of age; used or worn; the opposite of *new*
>The man is **old,** but the boy is young.
>Martha is eight years **old.**
>Ed wears **old** clothes when he paints.

on   over and touching; upon; at the time of
>The clown has a hat on his head.
>There is a picture **on** the wall.
>We left **on** Monday.

once   one time
>Please read the story **once** more.

on′ ion   *See* **Words for Vegetables,** page 201.

on′ ly   no more than one; just
>She is his **only** sister.
>I have **only** two dimes.

open   • fixed so that a person or a thing can go in or out; not closed
                   The door is **open.**
                   A bee flew through the **open** window.

                 • to move whatever is keeping a thing closed
                   You **open** and close your eyes.

opos' sum   *See* **Words for Animals,** page 208.

op' po site something which is in no way the same; the very different thing
                   Up is the **opposite** of *down.*

or   a word used between words or groups of words that offer a choice
                   Are you going by train **or** by bus?

or' ange   *See* **Words for Fruits,** page 199.

or' chard   the ground where fruit trees are grown
                   Many apple trees are growing in this **orchard.**

or' chid   *See* **Words for Flowers,** page 197.

oth' er   different from the one just spoken about
                   I live on one side of the street, and Patty lives on the **other** side.

our
ours
belonging to us; a form of *we*
    Our house is on a hill.
    The garage next to the house is also **ours.**

out
away from the inside; the opposite of *in;* at an end
    Mark is going **out** the door.
    Judy looked **out** the window.
    The fire is **out.**

out doors'
in the open air
    Today it is cooler **outdoors** than it is in the house.

out' side'
the outer part; the opposite of *inside*
    The **outside** of the box is blue.

over
above; across; to the other side
    A jet is flying **over** the city.
    Mother laid the blanket **over** the bed.
    The baby learned how to turn **over.**

own
• belonging to oneself
    Mary has her **own** bedroom.

• to have
    Do you **own** a bike?

pack

to put things together in a box or in a suitcase

    I will help you **pack** your bag.

    We **pack** our clothes before we go on a trip.

pack′ age

a bundle; things packed together

    A **package** came in the mail.

    Paul bought a **package** of gum.

paid

See **pay.**

pail

a round container with a handle for carrying things; a bucket

    Andy carried the **pail** of water.

paint

● solid color mixed with a liquid which dries after it has been spread on something

    I used a brush to spread the **paint.**

● to cover with color; to make a picture with paints

    Frank will **paint** the garage green.

    Many artists **paint.**

pair   two parts or things that go together
                  Mary has a **pair** of red shoes.

pal' ace   a large, fine house where a king and a
                  queen might live
                  The **palace** has beautiful gardens and
                  trees around it.

pan   a wide and not too deep dish, usually
                  made of metal
                  Mother put the cake **pan** in the oven.

pan' sy   *See* **Words for Flowers,** page 197.
pan' sies

pa' per   something to write on, to wrap things
                  with, and to make things from
                  We use a lot of **paper** in school.

pa rade'   a group of people marching
                  A band is leading the Fourth of July
                  parade.

park   • land set aside to be used for picnics and
                  fun
                  There are benches in the city **park.**

                  • to leave a car for a while
                  Father will **park** near the post office.

part a piece that is less than the whole
You may have **part** of my apple.

par' ty a group of people having fun together
par' ties The children are having fun at the birthday **party.**

pass to go by
pass' es I **pass** the fire station on my way to school.
The bus **passes** our house.

past gone by
In the spring winter is **past.**
It is **past** three o'clock.

paste something, such as flour and water, used to stick pieces of paper together
Betty spread **paste** on the back of the picture before she stuck it in her folder.

pas' ture a grassy field where cattle, horses, sheep, and other animals feed
Cattle graze in the **pasture.**

path a trail which has been made by people or animals walking
We followed the **path** up the hill.

paw   the foot of an animal which has claws
                   A dog has four **paws.**

pay   to give money for things bought or for
 paid   work done
 pay' ing   Father will **pay** the paper boy.
                       I **paid** twenty cents for the ice cream
                   cone.
                       The man is **paying** a bill at the store.

peach   See **Words for Fruits,** page 199.
 peach' es

pear   See **Words for Fruits,** page 199.

peas   See **Words for Vegetables,** page 201.

peep   to look through a small hole or a crack
                       John tried to **peep** through the crack
                   in the high fence.

peep   the small cry of a bird or a chick
                       Baby chickens **peep.**

pen   a tool used for writing with ink
                       I like to write with a **pen.**

pen   a closed yard for animals
                       A farmer often keeps his chickens in
                   a **pen.**

pen′ cil   a tool to write or to draw with
          I sharpened the point on my **pencil.**

pen′ guin   *See* **Words for Animals,** page 208.

pen′ ny   a one-cent coin
pen′ nies   Bonnie paid a **penny** for a piece of
          candy.

peo′ ple   human beings; men, women, and children
          People around the world use different
          languages.
          Many **people** are waiting for the bus.

pep′ per   *See* **Words for Vegetables,** page 201.

pet   an animal which is tamed and treated with
          love
          My **pet** is a rabbit.

pe tu′ nia *See* **Words for Flowers,** page 197.

pick   to choose; to take, as from a plant
          Kevin will **pick** the next story.
          May we **pick** some blueberries?

pic′ nic   an outing to which people bring food to
          eat in the open air
          The children fixed a basket of food to
          take on the **picnic.**

pic′ ture   a drawing; a painting; a photograph
    Beth drew a **picture** with crayons.
    At school there is a **picture** of George Washington.
    Dick has used his camera to take a **picture.**

pie   a pastry which is filled with something, such as fruit or meat, and baked
    Mother made a cherry **pie.**

piece   a part; a bit
    A **piece** of the puzzle is missing.
    May I have a **piece** of candy?
    Jerry found a **piece** of chalk.

pig   *See* **Words for Animals,** page 208.

pile   many things heaped together
    There is a **pile** of coats on the bed.
    Miss Hill put the papers in a **pile.**

pi′ lot   one who steers a plane or a ship
    The **pilot** landed the airplane on the runway.
    The **pilot** steered the steamboat.

pine′ ap ple   *See* **Words for Fruits,** page 199.

pipe   a tube through which something, such
as water or gas, can flow; a tube of wood,
clay, or metal with a bowl at one end
which is filled with tobacco

A water **pipe** is fastened under the
sink.

That man smokes a **pipe.**

place   ● a certain spot; a city, town, state, or
country

My bookmark marks the **place** where
I stopped reading.

What **places** did you see on your trip?

● to put or to set in a certain spot

plac′ ing   You may **place** the dishes here.

She is **placing** the flowers in a vase.

plan′ et   a heavenly body that moves around the
sun

Our earth is a **planet.**

plant   ● a living thing, such as a tree, a vegetable,
or a flower; any living thing that is not
an animal

A tree is a large **plant.**

Most **plants** have roots, stems, and
leaves.

● to put seeds or the roots of a plant into
the ground

We **plant** seeds in flowerpots.

plate

a dish, almost flat and usually round, on which food is served; a flat marker used as home base in baseball

Mother put the cookies on a **plate.**

The batter stands at home **plate.**

play

to have fun; to take part in; to make music with

The children **play** in the yard.

Tom and Al **play** baseball after school.

Ann can **play** the piano.

pleas' ant
pleas' ant ly

pleasing

The **pleasant** grocer talked with the people in his store.

A breeze is **pleasant** on a hot day.

The girl spoke **pleasantly.**

please

• a polite word you use when you ask for something

Please help me.

• to make glad

We **please** Mother when we help her.

plum

See **Words for Fruits,** page 199.

pock' et

a small bag which is sewed in clothing for carrying small things

Sandra put a handkerchief in her **pocket.**

poin set' tia   *See* **Words for Flowers**, page 197.

point   ● a sharp end
         The pencil has a fine **point.**

         ● to show a place or a direction, often by means of the finger
         Ted will **point** to the correct answer on the chalkboard.

pole   a long, slender, and often rounded piece of wood or metal
         The man is climbing the telephone **pole.**

po lice' man   a man whose job it is to keep order
po lice' men   in a city, town, or state by seeing that people obey the laws
         A **policeman** helped a lost girl find her home.

pond   a body of water which is smaller than a lake
         We watched some ducks swimming in the **pond.**

po' ny   *See* **Words for Animals**, page 208.
po' nies

pool a tank of water to swim in; a small pond
There are often swimming races at the **pool.**

poor having few things or little money;
poor' ly needing to be made better
After I lost my money, I was **poor.**
Corn will not grow in **poor** soil.
Donald writes **poorly.**

pop to break or to open with a short, quick
popped sound
pop' ping The balloon will **pop** if you stick a pin in it.
The popcorn **popped** in the hot pan.
Firecrackers were **popping.**

pop' py See **Words for Flowers,** page 197.
pop' pies

post a piece of wood or iron set in the ground
to support something
A sign is nailed to the **post.**

post' man a man whose job it is to deliver and to pick
post' men up letters and packages that are sent
through the mail
The **postman** left two letters in our mailbox.

pot   a deep, often heavy dish which is used to hold food or plants
           A **pot** of soup is on the stove.

po ta′ to   *See* **Words for Vegetables,** page 201.
po ta′ toes

pound   to strike hard
           Can you feel your heart **pound**?

pound   a measure of weight
           There are sixteen ounces in a **pound.**

pour   to cause to flow in a steady stream; to flow in a steady stream
           I'll **pour** the water into the glasses.
           During a storm the rain sometimes **pours** out of the sky.

pres′ ent   here; now
           All of the children are **present.**
           At **present** you are reading a page in a dictionary.

pres′ ent   a gift; something given
           I made a **present** for my mother.

pres′ i dent   the leader or the person in the highest office of a club or a nation
           We elected Max **president** of our club.

pret′ ty   pleasing to see or to hear
  pret′ ti er   Mother's pink hat is **pretty.**
  pret′ ti est   Do you think a rose is **prettier** than a dandelion?
    That is the **prettiest** song I know.

price   the amount of money for which a thing is bought or sold
    The **price** of the shirt is two dollars.

prince   the son of a king or a queen
    The king's son is a **prince.**

prin′ cess   the daughter of a king or a queen
    The prince's sister is a **princess.**

prize   something given for being the best in a race or a contest
    A **prize** was given to the winner.

proud   thinking well of oneself or of others
  proud′ ly   Jim felt **proud** when he won the prize.
    Mother said, "I am **proud** of you."
    Father smiled **proudly.**

pud′ dle   a small pool of water which is often dirty
    After it rained, there was a big **puddle** by the sidewalk.

pull	to move towards oneself with force; to tug

If you **pull** the handle, the wagon will move after you.

I **pull** my boots on over my shoes.

The baby likes to **pull** my hair.

pump′ kin   *See* **Words for Vegetables,** page 201.

pup′ pet   a small figure of a person or an animal which is moved by wires or the hands

The **puppet** moves if someone pulls the strings.

Janet made a hand **puppet.**

pup′ py   *See* **Words for Animals,** page 208.
pup′ pies

push   to press against something to move it
push′ es   away from you

The men are trying to **push** the car out of the snowdrift.

The little tug **pushes** the boat.

put   to place or to lay in a certain place
put   The girls will **put** their coats on.
put′ ting   I **put** my toys away before I went to bed.

Father is **putting** the car in the garage.

quack   to make the sound of a duck
          Ducks **quack** noisily.

quar' rel   to argue; to talk angrily
          Marcia and June may **quarrel** about which game to play.
          I saw a baseball player **quarrel** with the umpire.

quart   a measure
          Mother buys milk by the **quart.**
          A **quart** is one quarter of a gallon.

quar' ter   a part equal to one-fourth of the whole; a piece of money equal to twenty-five cents, or one-fourth of a dollar
          I ate a **quarter** of the orange.
          Two dimes and a nickel are the same amount of money as a **quarter.**
          A **quarter** is less than a half-dollar.

queen   a woman ruler; the wife of the king
          The **queen** lives in a palace.
          The people cheered their **queen.**

queer   odd; strange

> The book is about a **queer** little elf.
>
> Jim had a **queer** look on his face after tasting the lemon.

ques′ tion   a sentence which is asked when one is trying to find an answer

> Bill answered every **question** on the test.
>
> I want to ask a **question.**

quick   fast
  quick′ ly

> The trip to the city was **quick.**
>
> Come **quickly,** or we will be late.

qui′ et   without noise; very still; the opposite of
  qui′ et ly   *loud*

> The house is **quiet** when everyone is asleep.
>
> The baby played **quietly.**

quilt   A bedcover, usually made of two pieces of cloth sewed together with a soft lining between them

> Grandmother made a pretty **quilt** for my bed.

quite   really; completely or fully

> It is **quite** cold today.
>
> The paint is sticky, because it is not **quite** dry.

rab' bit   *See* **Words for Animals,** page 208.

rac coon'   *See* **Words for Animals,** page 208.

race   to run to try to beat; to go fast
   rac' ing   I will **race** you to the tree.
          Fire engines **race** to a fire.
          How many sailboats are **racing**?

ra' dio   a way of sending and receiving sounds by electrical waves without the use of connecting wires; the set which receives radio waves and gives out the sounds
      People get news by **radio.**
      We have a small white **radio** in our kitchen.

rain   drops of water falling from the clouds
   rainy   People carry umbrellas to keep from getting wet in the **rain.**
      Rain helps plants to grow.
      There are often dark clouds on **rainy** days.

raise
rais′ ing

to lift; to put up; to make grow

We **raise** our hands to talk in class.

The custodian **raises** the flag in front of our school.

Some farmers **raise** vegetables.

The wind is **raising** a lot of dust.

rake

- a tool which has a long handle with a row of teeth at one end for moving dirt, grass, or leaves

  Jack was using a **rake.**

- to gather or to smooth with a rake

rak′ ing

We **rake** leaves in the fall.

The boy is **raking** the garden.

ran

See **run.**

ranch
ranch′ es

a large farm where animals, such as cattle, sheep, and horses, are raised

There are many cattle being raised on this **ranch.**

rang

See **ring.**

rasp′ ber ry   *See* **Words for Fruits,** page 199.
  rasp′ ber ries

rat

See **Words for Animals,** page 208.

rat′ tle   to make many short, sharp sounds
  rat′ tling   When you shake the tin bank, the pennies **rattle.**
    The wind is **rattling** the windows.

reach   to touch; to get to; to stretch
  reach′ es   Susan can **reach** the top shelf.
    How long does it take you to **reach** school?
    My arm **reaches** above Aunt Betty's head.

read   to get the meaning of letters, words, and
read   signs which are written or printed; to say
  read′ ing   aloud what is written or printed
    I like to **read** sports stories.
    Jean has **read** the thermometer.
    Miss Ames is **reading** a letter to the children.

ready   prepared
    We cannot eat until dinner is **ready.**

real   true
    Is the story **real** or make-believe?

re′ al ly   truly
    She is **really** a girl, not a witch.
    The moon seems small, but it is **really** very large.

re mem′ ber   to keep in mind; to be able to think of
again
> Can you **remember** the answer?
> I wish I could **remember** her name.

rhi noc′ er os   *See* **Words for Animals,** page 208.

rich   having much of something
> The **rich** king had much gold.
> Cream has a **rich** taste.
> Plants grow well in **rich** soil.

rid′ dle   a question or a problem that is puzzling
> Can you guess the answer to the
> **riddle**?

ride   to be carried on or in something that
rode   moves, such as a horse or a car
rid′ den   > Cowboys **ride** horseback.
rid′ ing   > The boys **rode** their bicycles to school.
> Have you ever **ridden** a camel?
> Carol is **riding** in the back seat.

right   a direction; the opposite of *left;* good;
correct; the opposite of *wrong*
> Tim is writing with his **right** hand.
> We made a **right** turn at the corner.
> It is **right** to be kind and honest.
> Did Don have the **right** answer?

ring a circle of metal which sometimes has a stone set in it; a circle

Mother wears a **ring** on her finger.
Horses walked into the circus **ring**.
The children held hands and stood in a **ring** to play the game.

ring
rang
rung
ring′ ing

to make a clear sound, such as with a bell
Telephones **ring**.
Ted **rang** the bell on his bicycle.
Has the school bell **rung**?
The doorbell is **ringing**.

riv′ er a large, flowing stream of water

The **river** flows into the ocean.
The bridge crosses the **river**.

road a long, open way to travel on

There are many cars on the **road**.
A dirt **road** leads to the beach.

roar to make a loud noise

Lions **roar**.

rock a hard mass found in the ground

The hard part of the earth's surface is **rock**.
Terry found a big **rock** on the lawn.

rock   to move backward and forward or sideways

You can **rock** in this kind of chair.

The waves **rock** the boat.

rode   *See* **ride.**

ro′ deo   a contest of skill in such things as roping cattle and riding horses

Cowboys rode horses at the **rodeo.**

roll   • a kind of bread or cake

Peggy ate a hot **roll.**

• to move by turning over many times; to make flat with a roller

Ben will **roll** the tire into the garage.

The dog likes to **roll** in the grass.

Mother must **roll** the dough for a pie.

roof   the covering on the top of a building

There is a chimney on the **roof** of this building.

room   a space enclosed by walls in a house or a building; space

This **room** has one door and three windows.

There is **room** for you in the car.

root the part of a plant, usually in the soil, which feeds the plant and holds it in place
A carrot is a **root.**
The **roots** of most trees grow deep in the ground.

rope a thick, strong cord made of strings twisted together
The boat is tied to the dock with heavy **rope.**
I have a jump **rope.**

rose *See* **Words for Flowers,** page 197.

rot′ ten spoiled; weak
Jack could not eat the apple, because it was **rotten.**
The old steps are dangerous, because some of the boards are **rotten.**

round having a shape like a ball or a ring
A baseball is **round.**
A wheel is **round.**
I drew a clown with a **round** face.

row a line
Children are sitting in the front **row** of chairs.
The flowers grew in a **row.**

row

to move a boat with oars
Sam can **row** a boat.
He must pull hard on the oars when he **rows.**

rub′ ber

one of the low-cut coverings worn over the shoes to protect them from water; a stretch material
Jan wears her **rubbers** when it rains.
Tires and erasers are made of **rubber.**
Rubber is made from the juice of a tree.

rul′ er

a straight strip that is used in measuring; one who controls something, such as a country and its people
A **ruler** is usually twelve inches long.
The king was a wise **ruler.**

run
　ran
　run
　run′ ning

to move fast on the legs; to go
The boys can **run** fast.
A dog **ran** after the children.
Bob has **run** in a race.
The clock is not **running.**

rush
　rush′ es

to move fast; to hurry
I sometimes **rush** to the bus stop.
A person who is late often **rushes.**

sad
  sad' ly

unhappy
  The **sad** little girl began to cry.
  She looked **sadly** at the broken doll.

sad' dle

a seat, usually made of leather, for the rider on a horse or a bicycle
  The cowboy will put the **saddle** on the horse.

safe
  safe' ly

free from danger
  Carl keeps his money in a **safe** place.
  The men fixed the old bridge so that it would be **safe.**
  The airplane landed **safely.**

said

See **say.**

sail

● the cloth on a boat against which the wind blows to move the boat on the water
  The wind puffs out the **sail** on the small boat.

● to travel on water by boat
  In the summer people **sail** on the lake.

salt
salty

a white grain-like seasoning for foods, which is found in the earth and in sea water

    Jane filled the shaker with **salt.**

    The **salty** peanuts made me thirsty.

same

just alike; not different

    The boy's shirts are the **same** color.

    Jim's birthday is on the **same** day as mine.

sang

See **sing.**

sat

See **sit.**

sat' el lite

a heavenly body that moves around a larger body; a man-made object which is sent into orbit in space

    The moon is the earth's **satellite.**

    A man-made **satellite** may carry a camera to take pictures of outer space.

    Some **satellites** send messages.

save
sav' ing

to get someone or something out of danger; to keep or to put aside

    Lifeguards often **save** people who are drowning.

    I will **save** the candy to eat later.

    Judy is **saving** her money.

saw   a tool with sharp teeth that is used for cutting

Father uses a **saw** to cut the tree trunk into logs.

saw   *See* **see.**

say   to speak; to tell
  said   Please **say** that poem again.
  say' ing   "Dinner is ready," **said** Mother.
What is the man **saying**?

scare   to make afraid
  scar' ing   Do ghost stories **scare** you?
Our dog is **scaring** the little girl.

school   a place for teaching and learning

In **school** our teacher helps us learn many things.

We go to **school** five days a week.

scream   to cry out in a loud, sharp way

People sometimes **scream** when they are afraid or hurt.

sea   a large body of water; the ocean

The **sea** is salty.

seal   *See* **Words for Animals,** page 208.

seat   something to sit on, such as a chair or a bench

There is an empty **seat** in the first row.

se' cret   something which is known by one or two people, but kept from others

Barbara won't tell anyone the **secret.**

see   to sense through the eyes; to look at
saw   If you open your eyes, you can **see.**
seen   Andy **saw** dark clouds, and then he
see' ing   heard thunder.

Paula has **seen** the kittens.

We are **seeing** many new places.

seed   the small part of a plant from which new plants grow

I planted a **seed** in some dirt, and now the plant is starting to grow.

seem   to look to be

Does Bill **seem** better?

He **seems** happier today.

sell   to give for a price
sold   The woman **sells** flowers.
sell' ing   Tom **sold** his old skates for a dollar.

We are **selling** tickets to the school play.

send   to cause to go
  sent   I will **send** you a letter.
  send' ing   Aunt Anna **sent** Mark to the store.
             We are **sending** the letter by airmail.

set   ● a group
             Mother has a **set** of blue dishes.

         ● to put in place
set   I'll **set** the dishes on the table.
set' ting   Jeff **set** the box by the door before he
left.
             The gardener is **setting** plants in the
ground.

sev' er al   two or more, but not many
             The team has won **several** games.

shade   a somewhat dark place which is not in the
  shady   sunshine
             Let's sit in the **shade** under the big
tree.
             It is cooler under the **shady** tree than
it is in the bright sun.

shad' ow   shade made by a person, an animal, or
some object blocking out the sun or light
             The flagpole casts a long **shadow** on
the grass.

shake   to move up and down or back and forth
shook   I'll **shake** my beach towel to get the
shak′ en   sand out.
shak′ ing   Diane **shook** the jar of orange juice.
        Mrs. Paul has **shaken** the dusty mop.
        Tim was **shaking** his head to mean *no*.

shall   I **shall** come if I can.
should   He **shall** go to bed early even though
he doesn't want to.
        Jim asked if he **should** write his cousin
a letter.

shark   *See* **Words for Animals,** page 208.

sharp   having a fine cutting edge or a thin point;
sharp′ ly   like a knife
        The **sharp** knife cuts the meat easily.
        The cold wind feels **sharp** against my
cheeks.
        The angry woman spoke **sharply.**

she   the girl, the woman, or the female animal
her   spoken about
her   **She** is my aunt.
hers   I am visiting **her.**
        I am staying at **her** house.
        The green house is **hers.**

sheep   *See* **Words for Animals,** page 209.
sheep

shell

the hard covering on such things as some animals, birds' eggs, and nuts

Jim found a clam's **shell** at the beach.

A turtle can pull his head and his legs into his **shell.**

A robin's egg has a blue **shell.**

The **shell** of a nut is often hard.

shine
shone or
shined
shin' ing

to be bright with light; to make bright

Stars **shine** on a clear night.

I can **shine** shoes well.

The sun **shone** all day.

Beth is **shining** the silver.

shiny

bright

A new penny is **shiny.**

ship

an object which is larger than a boat and which is used for traveling on deep water

The sailor went to sea on a **ship.**

shirt

a piece of clothing worn on the upper part of the body by boys and men

A **shirt** usually has sleeves and a collar.

shoe

a covering for the foot, usually made of leather

A **shoe** fits the shape of a foot.

shook   *See* **shake.**

shoot   to hit with something, such as an arrow
  shot   or a bullet; to move out rapidly
  shoot' ing   In the movies cowboys may **shoot**
        at each other.
        Flames **shot** from the fire.
        The men were **shooting** arrows.

shop   • a store where things are sold
        My sister works in a flower **shop.**
        The bakery **shop** has pies for sale.

    • to look at or to buy things in a store
  shopped   People **shop** for food and clothes.
  shop' ping   Mother **shopped** at the supermarket.
        Cynthia was **shopping** for a hat.

shore   the land at the edge of a body of water
        It is rocky along this **shore.**

short   low; not tall; quick; not long
        The grass has been cut **short.**
        The class went for a **short** walk.

shot   *See* **shoot.**

should   *See* **shall.**

shout   to call in a loud voice

Since Steve is far away, he must **shout** if we are to hear him.

shov′ el   a tool which has a handle and a wide piece or scoop used to dig and throw

Ann dug into the sand with the **shovel**.
Bob used a **shovel** to lift the snow.

show   • a display or a program which can be seen, such as on television or on the stage

What television **show** do you watch?

• to let others look at; to be seen; to teach by doing

showed   Will you **show** us your goldfish?
shown or   The rip in her dress **showed**.
  showed   Mother has **shown** me how to knit.
show′ ing   Dick is **showing** his paper to Dan.

show′ er   a small amount of rain; a bath using a spray of water

The weatherman said there might be a **shower** today.
Sometimes I wash my hair when I take a **shower**.

sick   ill; not feeling well

Tommy is **sick** with the mumps.

side   an outer line or surface of an object; one of the two parts of something which is not the top, the bottom, the front, or the back; a certain part or place

> The figure in the picture has three **sides.**
>
> A bus has a door on one **side.**
>
> We play on this **side** of the street.

sign

● a mark or a message that points out or means something

> Here is a *For Sale* **sign.**
>
> The dark clouds were a **sign** of rain.
>
> We use the $ **sign** to stand for *dollar.*

● to write your own name on

> People **sign** their letters.

sig′ nal   an action, a word, or a sign that has a special meaning

> The man blew a whistle as a **signal** for the race to begin.

sil′ ly   foolish
sil′ lier
sil′ liest

> Jack looked **silly** in his sister's hat.
>
> My picture is **sillier** than yours.
>
> That is the **silliest** show I have seen.

sil′ ver   a shiny white metal

> Is your bracelet made of **silver**?
>
> **Silver** often shines brightly.

sing   to make musical sounds with the voice
  sang   The children **sing** well.
  sung   The bird **sang** sweetly.
  sing′ ing   We have **sung** this song many times.
                    Tom is **singing.**

sis′ ter   a girl or a woman who has the same
                  mother and father as another person
                      I have one **sister** and two brothers.

sit   to be in a seat
  sat   May I **sit** in the chair next to you?
  sit′ ting   On the bus trip, Mother **sat,** but I
                  stood.
                      The cat is **sitting** in a basket.

skate   ●a form for the foot with a metal blade on
                  the bottom for gliding on ice; a form for
                  the foot with rollers on the bottom for
                  gliding on hard, dry places
                      The blade on an ice **skate** is thin.
                      My roller **skates** have straps that go
                  around the tops of my shoes.

                  ●to glide while wearing ice skates or roller
                  skates
  skat′ ing   The children **skate** on the ice-covered
                  pond.
                      It is spring, and girls are **skating** on
                  the sidewalk.

skunk   *See* **Words for Animals,** page 209.

sky   the space above the earth
   skies   A clear **sky** is helpful to pilots.
        Stars twinkle in the night **sky.**

sled   a frame which is on runners and which is
        used for sliding on snow
             Robert will ride his **sled** down the
        snowy hill.

sleep   to rest the mind and the body
   slept   People usually close their eyes when
   sleep′ ing they **sleep.**
                   Who **slept** in my bed?
                   Timothy is **sleeping** now.

sleepy   needing sleep; tired
             Mother put the **sleepy** girl to bed.

slide   to move easily and quickly
   slid   Sam likes to **slide** down the long slide
   slid′ ing   at the playground.
                   Ed **slid** on the slippery floor.
                   The children are **sliding** on the ice.

slip′ pery   causing one to slide and maybe to fall
             A **slippery** floor can be dangerous.

slow   taking a long time; behind time
  slow′ ly   Since Brad is **slow** in getting ready,
              he is often late.
                    My watch is **slow.**
                    The old man walked **slowly.**

small   little; not large
                    The baby seems **small** next to his
              father.
                    My shoes are too **small.**

smart   quick to learn
                    Kay is **smart,** and she does good work.

smell   to sense with the nose
                    Do you **smell** something burning?

snail   *See* **Words for Animals,** page 209.

snake   *See* **Words for Animals,** page 209.

snow   frozen water in soft white flakes of
  snowy   different shapes
                    Snow fell from the wintry sky.
                    I wear my mittens on **snowy** days.

so   in such a way; very; and for that reason
                    Please do not talk **so** loud.
                    I am **so** sorry!
                    It rained, **so** that he could not go.

soft
soft′ ly   not hard or stiff; pleasing to touch; gentle
         My pillow is **soft.**
         A kitten's fur feels very **soft.**
         Our teacher has a **soft** voice.
         The mother sang **softly** to her baby.

sold   *See* **sell.**

sol′ id   not hollow; hard
         The block of wood is **solid.**

some   a certain, but not named, being or thing;
         a number of; any
         Some day next week Janet will visit us.
         Some plants bloom, but others do not.
         Do you want **some** food?

song   music to be sung
         Miss Snow played the piano while the
         children sang the **song.**

soon   in a short time; quickly
         We will come again **soon.**
         As **soon** as Mary comes, we will go.

sor′ ry   sad
         I am **sorry** that you are ill.

sound   something received through the sense of
         hearing
         Jean heard the **sound** of footsteps.

soup   a liquid food which is made by boiling such things as meat, fish, and vegetables in water
            This **soup** is too hot to eat.

south   a direction
            South is the opposite of *north*.
            Mexico is **south** of the United States.

space   a place; an endless area
            There is **space** in the car for you.
            The planets move through **space.**

speak   to talk; to use the voice
  spoke   You should **speak** clearly.
  spo′ ken   An author **spoke** to our class.
  speak′ ing   Mother has **spoken** to my teacher.
            Andy is **speaking** in front of an audience.

spend   to pay out; to use up
  spent   David will **spend** a nickel for an apple.
  spend′ ing   Kathy **spent** an hour at the library.
            The woman is **spending** money at the grocery store.

spi′ der   *See* **Words for Animals,** page 209.

spin′ ach   *See* **Words for Vegetables,** page 201.

splash
splash′ es

to cause water to fly about
Chris likes to **splash** in the bathtub.
The rain **splashes** on the window.

spoke

See **speak.**

spot

a mark; a place
There is a **spot** of ink on the shirt.
The cat found a good **spot** for a nap.

spread

to cover a wide area
If the milk spills, it may **spread** across
the table.

spring

the season between winter and summer;
a small stream of water that bubbles out
of the ground; an elastic part, usually
metal, which will return to its first shape
after it has been forced out of shape
Spring follows winter.
Water bubbled from the **spring.**
A **spring** under the car seat is broken.

squash

See **Words for Vegetables,** page 201.

squir′ rel

See **Words for Animals,** page 209.

stair

one of several steps which are used to go
from one level or one floor to another
The kitten is on the bottom **stair.**

stand
stood
stand' ing

to be in place on one's feet

We **stand** in line for the fire drill.

The children **stood** up to salute the flag.

At the game some people are sitting, but the boys are **standing.**

star

a heavenly body which appears bright at night; a shape; a performer who is very good

Have you ever seen the North **Star**?

In the movie the sheriff was wearing a silver **star.**

Bill Jones is the **star** of the school play.

start

to begin to go or to do

Mother will **start** cooking dinner soon.

The car won't **start.**

sta' tion

a stopping place for a bus or a train

This is a bus **station.**

Trains stop at the train **station.**

stay

to remain in one place

How long can you **stay**?

steam

water in the form of gas

Steam is coming from the pan of boiling water.

step
stepped
step′ ping

to move the foot from one place to another; to walk

Don't **step** in the mud puddle.
Tommy **stepped** on a bug.
Sam is **stepping** over the box.

stick

a thin piece of wood; a thin piece

The boys gathered **sticks** for the fire.
Paul chewed a **stick** of gum.

stick
stuck
stick′ ing

to push a pointed end into something; to make or to be hard to move

The sharp pin may **stick** you.
Lenny **stuck** a tack into the wall.
Is the stamp **sticking** to the envelope?

still

without moving or making noise

We sat **still** during the movie.

sting
stung
sting′ ing

to hurt with a pricking feeling

Smoke makes my eyes **sting**.
A wasp **stung** Don.
The burn on my finger is **stinging**.

stir
stirred
stir′ ring

to mix; to move

The painter must **stir** the paint.
No one **stirred** while Miss Long was out of the room.
Aunt Mary is **stirring** the soup.

stone   a piece of rock
                    We have a fireplace made of **stone.**

stood   *See* **stand.**

stop   to keep from moving; to come to an end
  stopped   The policeman will **stop** the cars to
stop' ping   let us cross the street.
                         It was quiet after the noise **stopped.**
                         The umpire is **stopping** the game
                    because it is raining.

store   a place where many things are kept to
                    sell
                         Jack bought a cap at the department
                    store.

storm   bad weather with strong wind and usually
  stormy   rain, hail, or snow
                         The wind blew hard during the **storm**
                    yesterday.
                         We play in the house on **stormy** days.

sto' ry   a telling of either true or made-up things
  sto' ries   and happenings
                         I read an interesting **story** about the
                    first space trip.

stove   an object which gets power from
something, such as gas or electricity, and
which is used for cooking and heating
> Mother took the pan of boiling water
off the **stove.**

straight   without a bend or a turn
> All the lines are **straight.**
> We went **straight** home.

strange   unusual; not known, heard, or seen before
> Pam had a **strange** dream.
> What is that **strange** animal?

stran' ger   one who is not known
> The **stranger** told people his name.

straw   a dried stem of a grain plant; a tube,
usually made of paper, through which
one can suck liquids
> Cattle often sleep on beds of **straw.**
> I sipped the soda through a **straw.**

straw' ber ry   *See* **Words for Fruits,** page 199.
straw' ber ries

street   a road in a town or city
> Many cars travel down our **street.**
> A city has many **streets.**

strike
  struck
  strik′ ing

to hit with force; to stop work as a group for a reason

    Strike the ball with the bat.

    The workers may **strike,** because they want better pay.

    A car **struck** a tree.

    The bus drivers are **striking.**

string

very thin rope; very heavy thread

    The package is tied with **string.**

    Betty is putting beads on a **string.**

strong

having power or force

    You must be **strong** to lift the trunk.

struck   *See* **strike.**

stuck   *See* **stick.**

stung   *See* **sting.**

sud′ den
  sud′ den ly

quick

    He made a **sudden** movement.

    Suddenly the wind began to blow.

sug′ ar

a sweetening, usually made from sugar cane or sugar beets

    I put some **sugar** in the lemonade.

suit   clothing worn by a man or a boy that is made up of a matching jacket, pants, and sometimes a vest; a woman's or a girl's matching jacket and skirt

Joe has a blue wool **suit.**

Miss Baker sometimes wears a **suit** instead of a dress.

sum' mer   the season between spring and fall

It is often hot in the **summer.**

sun   the heavenly body which gives us light
sun' ny   and heat

The **sun** is shining brightly.

Sunny days are cheerful.

sun' flow er   *See* **Words for Flowers,** page 197.

sup' per   an evening meal

When people eat dinner at noon, they have **supper** at night.

sup pose'   to think it is possible

Do you **suppose** the rain will stop?

sure   certain; without a doubt
sure' ly   I feel **sure** I can win the race.

That man is **surely** Mr. Thomas.

sur prise′   something unexpected
Mother has a **surprise** for us, and we are trying to guess what it is.

swan   *See* **Words for Animals,** page 209.

sweet   tasting like sugar; pleasant
Honey tastes **sweet.**
Roses have a **sweet** smell.
The baby has a **sweet** smile.

swim   to move oneself forward in the water
swam   without touching the ground or any
swum   bottom surface
swim′ ming   You move your arms and your legs when you **swim.**

The fish **swam** around in the fishbowl.
Have you ever **swum** in the ocean?
Ducks are **swimming** in the pond.

swing   to move back and forth
swung   People **swing** their arms when they
swing′ ing   walk.
The door **swung** open and then closed.
The monkey is **swinging** by his tail.

swish   to move with a hissing sound
swish′ es   Leaves often **swish** in the breeze.
The nurse's stiff dress **swishes** when she walks.

ta' ble a piece of furniture having a flat top on legs

The children sat at the **table** to eat their lunch.

tail a growth from the back of an animal; something like an animal's tail

The dog is wagging his **tail**.

I made a long **tail** of rags for my kite.

take to get; to go with; to use
  took May I **take** a cookie from the box?
  tak' en "Please **take** Sally outdoors," said
  tak' ing Mother.

They **took** a bus to the city.

Who has **taken** the last piece of candy?

We are **taking** John to the movies.

tale a story

I read a fairy **tale**.

talk to speak; to say words

You should listen when people **talk**.

tall   high
Some city buildings are very **tall**.
Henry was short, but he grew to be **tall**.

tap   to hit lightly
tapped   **Tap** gently on the door.
tap' ping   Rain **tapped** on the roof.
Who is **tapping** on the window?

taste   to get the flavor of something by putting
tast' ing   a small part of it in your mouth
Mother will **taste** the soup to see if it is too salty.
Peter is **tasting** the chocolate pudding.

taxi   an automobile with a special driver, which people pay to ride in
When we missed the bus, we had to take a **taxi** to school.
The ride in the **taxi** cost a dollar.

teach   to show how to do something; to lead
teach' es   others to learn
taught   I will **teach** you a new game.
teach' ing   My mother **teaches** the first grade.
Who **taught** you how to ride a bicycle?
Mrs. Blake is **teaching** our class many interesting facts about science.

team   a number of people working or playing together

>Our **team** won the game.

tear   to pull or to rip apart
  tore
  torn
  tear′ ing

>How did you **tear** your dress?
>Joe **tore** his shirt on a sharp nail.
>Someone has **torn** the book jacket.
>Louis is **tearing** up the old papers.

tear   a drop of salty water from the eye

>A **tear** ran down the baby's cheek.

teeth   *See* **tooth.**

tel′ e phone   a set which uses electricity to let people who are near or far apart talk to each other

>My cousin in Chicago called my aunt in Boston on the **telephone.**

tel′ e vi sion   a way of sending and receiving pictures and sounds by electrical waves; the set which receives the electrical waves and gives out the pictures and the sounds

>**Television** lets people see things that are happening far away.
>Bob turned on the **television** to watch the ball game.

tell   to say; to let others know
  told   I can't **tell** which book is yours.
  tell′ ing   Will you **tell** me the secret?
    Mother **told** Jim that it was time for
bed.
    Mrs. Parker is **telling** us a story.

tem′ per a ture   a measure of heat or cold
    When the air gets warmer, the
temperature changes.

tent   a movable shelter, usually made of cloth
and supported by poles in the ground
    Campers sometimes sleep in a **tent.**

than   when compared to
    I am older **than** Catherine.

thank   to say that one is pleased about
something said or done
    You should **thank** people when they
are kind to you.

that   pointing out someone or something
which is farther away or which has been
spoken about; which
    I will take **that** book, not this one.
    We can't stay **that** long.
    Joan ate the apple **that** was on the
table.

the   pointing out a certain one or ones
                    The boys raced down **the** road.

their
  theirs   belonging to them; a form of *they*
                    The boys took off **their** coats.
                    The coats on the hooks are **theirs.**

them   the persons, the animals, or the things spoken about; a form of *they*
                    Judy asked **them** to go with us.

then   at that time; soon afterward
                    Just **then** our doorbell rang.
                    I'll read the book, and **then** you may have it.

there   in that place
                    He sat **there,** instead of here.

these   pointing out persons or things which are nearby
                    Is one of **these** boys his brother?
                    These shoes are bigger than those shoes.

they
  them
  their   the persons, the animals, or the things spoken about
  theirs
                    They are the biggest boys on the team.
                    I live near **them.**
                    Their father is watching the game.
                    The caps on the grass are **theirs.**

thick having a great measure between sides; not thin; growing or being close together; like glue

The telephone book for a large city is very **thick.**

We had fun hiding in the long, **thick** grass.

The paint is too **thick** to use.

thin not thick or fat; growing far apart; like
thin′ ner water
thin′ nest Lisa is too **thin** to wear this skirt.

Grandfather has **thin** hair.

I made the paste **thinner** by adding water.

The **thinnest** book is not always the easiest to read.

thing an object; an idea; a happening

A desk is a **thing.**

Tim thought of an interesting **thing** to write about.

A funny **thing** happened today.

think to use the mind; to have an idea; to have
thought in mind
think′ ing People can **think,** but plants cannot.

Peggy **thought** of a game we could play.

Betty was **thinking** about vacation.

thirsty   wanting something to drink
        The dog is **thirsty** and needs some water.

this   pointing out a person or a thing which is nearby
        This football is Jim's, but that baseball is Andy's.
        This boy is my brother.

those   pointing out persons or things which are far away
        Those people across the street are my parents.
        Which of **those** dolls do you like?

thought   *See* **think.**

threw   *See* **throw.**

through   from one end to the other end of
        This road will take you **through** the city.

throw   to toss
  threw   You **throw** the ball, and I'll catch it.
  thrown   Alice **threw** the empty bag into the
  throw′ ing wastebasket.
        I have **thrown** the papers away.
        The children are **throwing** snowballs.

tick′ et a card or a piece of paper which lets one do something, such as go to a show or ride on a bus

Paul paid for the **ticket** to the game.

Do you have a bus **ticket**?

ti′ ger *See* **Words for Animals**, page 209.

tight not easily moved or undone; fitting closely; not loose

Ed can tie a **tight** knot in the rope.

My toes hurt, because my shoes are too **tight.**

time a measure of years, days, hours, and minutes; a part of a year, day, or hour

Clocks and calendars are two ways of telling **time.**

What **time** do you get to school?.

ti′ ny very small

ti′ ni er The kittens are **tiny.**

ti′ ni est They are **tinier** than the cat.

The gray kitten is the **tiniest** of the three kittens.

tip an end part which is rounded or pointed

The seal has a ball on the **tip** of his nose.

tip
tipped
tip′ ping

to turn over
    Canoes **tip** easily.
    Who **tipped** over the flowerpot?
    The glass is **tipping**!

tip

a small amount of money given to a
person for good service
    Mrs. Burns gave a **tip** to the taxi driver
who took her to the airport.

tire

a band of rubber or metal around a wheel
    Each wheel on my bicycle has a rubber
tire.

tired

worn out; sleepy
    After a long day at work, the men were
tired.

to

in the direction of; on; for
    Turn **to** the left.
    Does the stamp stick **to** the envelope?
    Jack has the key **to** the front door.

toad

See **Words for Animals,** page 209.

to day′

at the present time
    Today is between yesterday and
tomorrow.

to geth′ er   with each other; not alone
>The girls are walking **together.**
>Jack nailed the boards **together.**
>We sat **together** at lunchtime.

told   *See* **tell.**

to ma′ to   *See* **Words for Vegetables,** page 201.
  to ma′ toes

to mor′ row   the day after the present one
>Today is Saturday, and **tomorrow** will be Sunday.

to night′   the night of today
>I am sleepy **tonight.**

too   also; more than what is enough
>Jane is here, and Ann is, **too.**
>Mark is **too** young to go to school.

took   *See* **take.**

Crown

Root

tooth   one of the bony parts in the mouth which
  teeth   are used for biting; something like a tooth, such as on a comb or a saw
>A **tooth** has a root and a crown.
>Each **tooth** on the saw is sharp.

top   the highest part
          Snow covers the **top** of the mountain.
          Your head is at the **top** of your body.

top   a toy with a pointed end on which it spins
          The **top** turned round and round.

tore   *See* **tear.**

tor na' do   a very strong wind which whirls around
          like a cone-shaped cloud
          The **tornado** blew many trees down.

touch   to put the hand or some part of the body
touch' es   on something; to come against
          I can bend and **touch** my toes.
          The tree branch **touches** our roof.

toward   in the direction of
          They walked **toward** the park.
          The puppy raced **toward** the boys.

tow' er   a high, narrow building or a high, often
          narrow part of a building
          A clock is in the **tower.**
          The old castle had a stone **tower.**

town
a group of many houses and buildings, which is smaller than a city

There is less traffic in a **town** than in a city.

toy
a plaything

A puppet is a **toy.**

track
a row of metal rails for cars to run on; a mark made by a wheel or a foot passing over an area

The train **track** has steel rails.

The dog left muddy **tracks** on the rug.

trac′ tor
a heavy machine used to pull such things as plows and other machines

The **tractor** pulled our car out of the ditch.

trade
trad′ ing
to give one thing for another

Will you **trade** books with me?

We **trade** pictures of ballplayers.

Since Tim's chair is too small, he is **trading** it for Jack's bigger chair.

traf′ fic
the movement of people, cars, and bicycles along streets and roads

There is a lot of **traffic** on this road during the summer.

trail
- a path or a track
  The jet left a **trail** of gases in the sky.

- to follow
  Dogs often **trail** behind a parade.

train
- a line of railroad cars which are fastened together and pulled by an engine
  The **train** is coming down the track.

- to teach
  Bill can **train** his dog to do tricks.

trap
something used to catch animals
Father caught a mouse in the **trap.**

trav′ el
to go on a trip
We will **travel** in Canada this summer.

treas′ ure
riches which have been stored up or hidden
The boys pretended they were digging for **treasure** in the sand.

tree
a large, woody plant with a trunk, branches, and leaves
This is a maple **tree.**
A **tree** is the largest kind of plant.

trick   something done to fool people; a clever act

The magician's **trick** made us think that the glass had really disappeared.

Ted taught his dog a **trick** of begging for food.

trip   ● a journey

The class is taking a **trip** to the art museum.

The Greens went on a **trip** last year.

tripped
trip′ ping

● to stumble; to catch the foot and fall

You may fall if you **trip.**

Barbara **tripped** on the rock.

Dick was **tripping** over things in the dark room.

trot
trot′ ted
trot′ ting

to move like a horse by lifting a front foot and the opposite hind foot at the same time

We watched the horse **trot.**

The little dog **trotted** down the road.

The pony is **trotting** around the circus ring.

truck   a heavy automobile for carrying loads

The repairman put our broken T.V. into his **truck.**

The milkman drives a **truck.**

trunk the main stem of a tree, not including the branches and the roots; a large case; a space, often in the back of a car, for storing things; the long snout of an elephant

Bark covers the **trunk** of the tree.

We packed our clothes in a **trunk.**

Father keeps tools in the **trunk** of the car.

The elephant can use his **trunk** to hold things.

try to attempt
tries
tried
try′ ing

You should **try** to do your best.

The baby **tries** to walk.

I **tried** to open the door, but it was locked.

Frank is **trying** to go to sleep.

tug ● a small boat used to tow and to push larger boats

The little **tug** pushed the boat.

The large ship was towed into port by a **tug.**

● to pull hard
tugged
tug′ ging

The puppy likes to **tug** at the shoe.

We **tugged** on the rope which was tied to the boat.

Billy was **tugging** on the heavy wagon to make it move.

tu′ lip   *See* **Words for Flowers,** page 197.

tum′ ble   to fall or to turn over
  tum′ bling   If you run, you may **tumble** down
            the steps.
                 The clothes are **tumbling** about in the
            washing machine.

tur′ key   *See* **Words for Animals,** page 210.

turn   ● a change of direction; a chance or a time
            to do something
                 The car is making a **turn** to the right.
                 It is Alice's **turn** to swing.

            ● to move around; to change direction
                 When you are riding a bicycle, the
            wheels **turn** many times.
                 The bus will **turn** left at the corner.

tur′ nip   *See* **Words for Vegetables,** page 201.

tur′ tle   *See* **Words for Animals,** page 210.

twin   one of two children born at the same
            time to the same mother
                 Ellen is my **twin,** and we look alike.
                 Twins do not always look alike.

ug′ ly not pleasant to look at
 The unkind witch in the movie had an **ugly** face.

um brel′ la a folding frame covered with cloth and used to protect one from rain or sun
 The red **umbrella** is open, but the blue one is closed.
 The baby sat in the shade under the beach **umbrella.**

um′ pire a person who sees that the rules are followed in a game, such as baseball
 The **umpire** cried, "You're out!"

un′ cle the brother of one's father or one's mother; the husband of one's aunt
 My father's brother is my **uncle.**

un′ der below; lower than
 Ned Jones lives in an apartment **under** ours.
 As the boys watched from above, the boat sailed **under** the bridge.

un til'   up to the time when
                   Dan can stay **until** his father calls.

up   toward the top of; to a higher place
                   Louise is running **up** the stairs.
                   The helicopter began to go **up.**

up on'   on the top of
                   The puppy jumped **upon** the chair.

us   the person speaking and one or more
               persons spoken about; a form of *we*
                   John asked **us** to go camping.
                   His father helped **us** put up the tent.

use   to put into action or to work
us' ing   May I **use** your pen?
                   Bill is **using** Father's typewriter.

use' ful   helpful
                   Old lumber is **useful** for making many
               things.

usu al   common
usu al ly   It is not **usual** to have snow in Florida.
                   A policeman **usually** stands on the
               corner near school.

va ca′ tion   a time of fun and rest from work

We have a long **vacation** from school in the summer.

Father will have a two-week **vacation.**

val′ en tine   a card or a gift given to a friend or a loved one on St. Valentine's Day, February 14

Elizabeth pasted a red heart on the **valentine** she made for her mother.

val′ ley   the low land between hills or mountains

From the top of the hill, we could see the **valley** below.

A river flows through the **valley.**

vase   a holder for flowers

Miss Baker put the daisies in a green glass **vase.**

veg′ e ta ble   a plant having some part which is used for food

Beans are my favorite **vegetable.**

very   truly; greatly

Mrs. Gordon is a **very** kind woman.
The Statue of Liberty is **very** tall.

vil' lage   a small town

There are only a few stores in the **village.**

vi' o let   *See* **Words for Flowers,** page 197.

vis' it   to come or to go to see; to stay with

"Shall we **visit** Uncle Harry today?" asked Mrs. Howe.
My cousin may **visit** us for a week.

vis' i tor   one who goes to see a person or a place

George had many **visitors** when he was in the hospital.

voice   the sound which comes through the mouth of a person talking or singing

Father speaks in a deep **voice.**

vow' el   an open sound made by the voice; a letter of the alphabet that stands for an open sound made .by the voice

The letters *a, e, i, o,* and *u* are **vowels.**
Sometimes the letter *y* is a **vowel,** as in the word *bicycle.*

wag' on

a four-wheeled cart for carrying loads
Robert is putting the bag into the **wagon.**
The horses pulled the farm **wagon.**

wait

to stop; to stay until someone comes or until something happens
"**Wait** for me," Jimmy called as he ran after the boys.
I will **wait** for the rain to stop.

walk

● a path or place for traveling, usually on foot
We played by the **walk** in front of our apartment building.

● to go by foot
Sam will **walk,** but I will ride.

wall

the side of a building or a room; something that encloses an area
One **wall** in the room is green.
A cat walked on the **wall** between our yard and the neighbor's yard.

wal′ rus   *See* **Words for Animals,** page 210.
   wal′ rus or **wal′ rus es**

want   to wish for; to need
     Mark and Jeff **want** summer to come.
     Do you **want** anything at the store?

warm   having some heat; more hot than cold
     Ann felt the **warm** sun on her back.

warn   to let one know ahead of time of a danger
or an unpleasant happening
     Did you **warn** the boys that the ice is
too thin to skate on?
     Weathermen **warn** us about storms.

was   a form that is used to show past time
(Use with *I, he, she, it,* and words that
mean only one.)
     I **was** in bed early last night.
     He **was** in Susan's class last year.
     Miss Smith **was** at school yesterday.
     The sun **was** shining.

wash   to clean with water or some other liquid
   wash′ es   You should **wash** your hands when
they are dirty.
     Mother **washes** our clothes in the
washing machine.

wasp   *See* **Words for Animals,** page 210.

watch   • a small clock, usually worn on the wrist
  watch′ es   A **watch** is often run by a small spring.

             • to pay attention to; to look at
                We **watch** our teacher when she is
explaining something to us.
                Ron **watches** television after dinner.

wa′ ter   the liquid that fills lakes, oceans, and
rivers and comes from the sky as rain
                People use **water** for drinking and
washing.
                Land and **water** cover the earth.

wa′ ter mel on *See* **Words for Fruits,** page 199.

wave   • a moving ripple of water; moving energy
in the air, such as sound or light
                A **wave** splashed against the side of
the boat.
                Sound travels through the air by
means of **waves.**

             • to move something, such as the hand,
up and down or back and forth
  wav′ ing   People **wave** good-by to each other.
                The boy is **waving** his hand.

way   direction; plan; distance
    Which **way** should we go?
    I thought of a new **way** to play the game.
    It is a long **way** from my house to your house.

we
  us
  our
  ours   the person who is speaking and one or more persons
    We are glad you came.
    You should visit **us** often.
    Have you seen **our** new kittens?
    The dog is **ours,** too.

weak   not strong; easily broken
    Chris is too **weak** to lift the box.
    The baby's cries were **weak.**
    The **weak** bridge may break under the heavy truck.

wear
  wore
  worn
  wear' ing   to have on the body
    Sue will **wear** her blue jacket today.
    Miss Clark **wore** a flower on her suit.
    Has Alice **worn** that hat before?
    The man is **wearing** a red shirt.

weath' er   the condition of the air outside
    When the **weather** is stormy, the air is often windy and cool.
    On the desert the **weather** is hot and dry.

weave
wove
wo' ven
weav' ing

to make something, such as cloth, by putting threads over and under each other

The woman is using a loom to **weave** the cloth.

Raymond **wove** a basket from strips of straw.

The spider has **woven** a web.

I am **weaving** a potholder.

wee

very tiny

A hummingbird is a **wee** bird.

week

the seven days between Sunday and Saturday; any seven days, one right after another

Saturday is the last day of the **week.**

We will go to the game in a **week.**

weigh

to find out how heavy something is; to have as weight

You stand on the scales if you want to **weigh** yourself.

The suitcases **weigh** fifty pounds.

wel' come
wel' com ing

to greet or to receive happily

Our neighbors **welcome** us home after we have been away.

Jeff is **welcoming** the visitors.

well
bet′ ter
best

in a good way
>You did your work **well.**
>Al writes **better** than he did.
>Shirley writes **best** of all.

well

a hole dug in the ground to get gas, oil, or water
>Oil is being pumped from the **well.**
>The **well** is deep in the ground.

went

See **go.**

were

a form that is used to show past time (Use with *you, we, they,* and words that mean more than one.)
>You **were** at the party, and he was, too.
>We **were** sick, but they **were** in school.
>The children **were** reading.

west

a direction; where the sun seems to set
>*East* is the opposite of **west.**
>Follow the highway **west** of the city.

wet
wet′ ter
wet′ test

soaked or covered with water or another liquid; not dry
>My shoes are **wet.**
>Is the fresh paint still **wet**?
>His mittens are **wetter** than yours.
>This is the **wettest** month of the year.

whale

See **Words for Animals,** page 210.

wharf
wharves
or wharf

a platform along the shore where ships load and unload
   Boats stop alongside the **wharf** to unload and to pick up cargo.
   Boys fished from the **wharf.**

what

which thing or things; which
   What did you have for lunch?
   I asked Jill **what** book she read.

wheat

a grain from which flour, cereals, and other foods are made
   When **wheat** is ripening, it looks like long, golden grass.

wheel

a round frame that turns on a center pin
   A tricycle has three **wheels.**

when

at what time; at the time that
   When can you come?
   We will go **when** Tom comes.

where

at what place; in the place that
   Where do you live?
   Judy put the candy **where** it belongs.

which   what one; that
                 Which cap is yours?
                 I read the story **which** you wrote.

while   during the time that
                 I slept **while** it rained.
                 While Al was talking, we were quiet.

whip   to beat
  whipped   It is unkind to **whip** a dog.
  whip' ping   The rider lightly **whipped** the horse so
                 that it would go faster.
                     The rain is **whipping** against the sails.

whis' per   to speak in a soft voice
                     We must **whisper** so that we won't
                 awaken the baby.
                     Will you **whisper** the secret to me?

whis' tle   to make a shrill sound by blowing air
  whis' tling through a small opening
                     I can **whistle** many songs.
                     James was **whistling** while he was
                 walking to school.

who   what person or persons
  whom   **Who** did that?
  whose   To **whom** did you speak?
                     Whose jacket is this?

whole
having all its parts; not just a part of
The apple is **whole,** and the peach is cut into pieces.
We ate the **whole** pie.

why
for what reason
Why did you do that?
Tell me **why** you are crying.

wide
wide′ ly
having a great measure from side to side; not narrow
The board is **wide,** and the ruler is narrow.
The ocean is so **wide** that we can't see the other shore.
A famous person is **widely** known.

wife
wives
a married woman
Mother is Father's **wife.**

wild
wild′ ly
not tame; growing or being without direction
Animals in the jungle are **wild.**
Sometimes flowers grow **wild** along the railroad track.
The lion raged **wildly** in the cage.

will
would
I **will** go to school tomorrow.
Ann **will** sing a song in the show.
The boys **will** visit Pete.
He **would** have been gone by then.

win
won
win' ning

to do better than others in a game or a contest

The blue boat will **win** the race.
Jill **won** first prize in the art show.
We are **winning** the game.

wind
windy

moving air

The **wind** blows the clothes on the line.

Men must hold onto their hats on **windy** days.

wind
wound
wind' ing

to wrap around or to roll up; to turn a part of a machine to tighten the spring that makes it go

I'll **wind** the yarn into a ball.
Father **wound** his watch.
Alice is **winding** the string around the box.

win' dow

an opening in a wall which lets in light and usually air

Sunlight shines through the **window.**

wing

the part of a bird, a flying insect, or a bat which is needed for flying; any part which is like a wing, as on an airplane

A bird has two **wings.**
The toy airplane has a broken **wing.**

wink   to close and open one eye quickly, usually as a signal

Sometimes Grandfather will **wink** at me when he is joking.

win′ ter   the season between fall and spring

Last **winter** was very cold.

Some places have snow in the **winter.**

wire   a thin piece of metal which is like thread or cord

A bird is sitting on the telephone **wire.**

There are many electrical **wires** inside our television set.

wise
wise′ ly   having and showing good sense

You are **wise** to get a good night's sleep.

I try to spend my money **wisely.**

wish
wish′ es   to want

I **wish** I had a brother.

Mel **wishes** he lived in Colorado.

with   in the company of; by means of

Will you come **with** me?

I cut the bread **with** a knife.

wolf   *See* **Words for Animals,** page 210.
wolves

wom′ an   a grown-up girl
wom′ en   That **woman** is my aunt.

won′ der   to wish to know
                 Do you **wonder** what the surprise will
                 be?

won′ der ful very fine; strangely exciting
                 This is a **wonderful** party!
                 The astronauts must see **wonderful**
                 things in outer space.

wood   the hard part under the bark of trees,
                 which has many uses when cut
                 Tables and chairs are often made of
                 wood.

wood′ chuck *See* **Words for Animals,** page 210.

woods   many trees growing wild and close
                 together
                 Wildflowers bloom in the **woods.**
                 The **woods** do not grow as thick as a
                 forest.

wool
wool′ ly

the soft covering from a sheep which can be made into threads for cloth

Men cut the **wool** from the sheep.

My coat is made of **wool.**

The **woolly** blanket was heavy and warm.

word

a sound or a group of sounds which is made by the human voice and which has meaning; a letter or a group of letters which is written to stand for a sound or a group of sounds that has meaning

How many sounds can you hear in that **word**?

There are usually both vowels and consonants in a **word.**

wore

See **wear.**

work

anything which a person does to make a thing or to bring a plan to an end; a job or business

After I do my **work,** I can play.

Father leaves for **work** at seven o'clock.

world

the earth; the planet on which we live

Our **world** is very large.

The spacemen could see the **world** from their spaceship.

worm   *See* **Words for Animals,** page 210.

wor' ry   to be uneasy or troubled
  wor' ries   Mother may **worry** if we are not home
  wor' ried on time.
  wor' ry ing   Father **worries** about our old car.
            We **worried** about the sick boy.
            Are you **worrying** about the storm?

would   *See* **will.**

wound   *See* **wind.**

wreck   to break apart or to damage
            The workmen must **wreck** the old
building.
            Drivers must be careful, or they may
wreck their cars.

write   to make letters or words with a marker,
  wrote   such as a pen, a pencil, or chalk
  writ' ten   Laura will **write** her name on the top
  writ' ing line of the paper.
            The teacher **wrote** a sentence on the
chalkboard.
            Have you **written** a letter to Jane?
            Joe is **writing** a letter.

wrong   bad; not right; not as it should be
            It is **wrong** to tell a lie.
            Only one of my answers was **wrong.**

X ray a powerful ray which cannot be seen and which can go through things that light cannot; a picture, often of some area inside the body, which is taken by means of this ray

A special machine uses **X rays.**

The doctor showed us the **X ray** of a man's chest.

xy′ lo phone a musical instrument which is played with wooden hammers

This is a **xylophone.**

The boy knows how to play a song on the **xylophone.**

Can *you* think of any other words that begin with the letter **X**?

yard   a piece of ground around a house, a school, or some other building
We have a **yard** behind our house.
There is a set of swings in the **yard** at school.

yard   a measure of length
There are three feet in a **yard.**

yawn   to open the mouth wide when one is sleepy or bored
I **yawn** when I am tired.

year   the time from January 1 to December 31; any twelve months, one right after another
There are twelve months in a **year.**
The new school will be built in a **year.**

yell   to scream or to shout
We **yell** and cheer when our favorite team is winning.

yes   a word used in an answer to mean *that is right*
                "**Yes,** I can hear you," Margaret
        answered.
                Yes is the opposite of *no*.

yes′ ter day the day before today
                Yesterday was the last day of April,
        and today is the first day of May.

yet   at this time
                I hope you won't go **yet**.
                Is Jerry home from school **yet**?

you   the person or the persons spoken to
  you   **You** are reading a dictionary.
  your   Who gave it to **you**?
  yours   There are other children in **your** class.
                Which desk is **yours**?

young   in the first part of life
                Young is the opposite of *old*.
                A calf is a **young** cow.

your   belonging to you; a form of *you*
  yours   Is this **your** desk?
                This is my hat, and that is **yours**.

ze′ bra   *See* **Words for Animals,** page 210.

ze′ ro   0; nothing; the point between *1* and −*1* on a thermometer

If you add **zero** to one, you still have one.

The temperature is below **zero,** and the air feels very cold.

zig′ zag   having a shape of short, sharp turns

The jack-o′-lantern has a **zigzag** smile.

Cars go slowly along the **zigzag** road.

zoo   a place where animals are kept in cages or in fenced places so that people can see them

We like to see the lions in the **zoo.**

Word Lists
for
My Second Picture Dictionary

Words for the Space Age

aerospace	gravity	reentry
astronaut	launch pad	rocket
booster	lift-off	satellite
capsule	missile	spaceship
countdown	nose cone	space station
escape hatch	orbit	space suit
flight	outer space	thrust
gantry	recovery	weightlessness

Compound Words

airplane	highway	raincoat
baseball	home run	roller skate
basketball	homework	sailboat
bedroom	ice cream	sea horse
beehive	jack-in-the-box	seashore
classroom	jack-o'-lantern	shoemaker
cowboy	jump rope	shopkeeper
doorknob	lighthouse	sidewalk
firecracker	moonlight	snowball
fire escape	newspaper	stop sign
fireman	playground	sunshine
fishhook	police dog	toothache
football	policeman	traffic light
goldfish	postman	washing machine
good-by	post office	windshield
grown-up	railroad	workbook
high school	rainbow	wristwatch

Antonyms

(Word Opposites)

glad

sad

above	below	fat	thin
back	front	few	many
bad	good	first	last
beneath	over	frown	smile
closed	open	hard	soft
cold	hot	heavy	light
dark	light	long	short
dry	wet	loose	tight
dull	sharp	lose	win
early	late	new	old
empty	full	poor	rich
false	true	right	wrong
far	near	rough	smooth
fast	slow	short	tall

Homonyms

hair

hare

ate	eight		mail	male	
bare	bear		meat	meet	
be	bee		pair	pear	pare
blew	blue		peace	piece	
brake	break		red	read	
buy	by		right	write	
cent	scent	sent	sail	sale	
dew	do	due	sea	see	
fair	fare		sew	sow	so
hear	here		son	sun	
hour	our		tail	tale	
knew	new		their	there	
knot	not		threw	through	
made	maid		to	two	too

Kinds of Workers

artist

bricklayer

dentist

baker

chemist

doctor

banker

clerk

electrician

forest ranger

musician

teacher

judge

nurse

truck driver

mail carrier

plumber

veterinarian

Words for Flowers

aster

daffodil

hibiscus

carnation

daisy

Indian paintbrush

crocus

geranium

iris

marigold

poinsettia

sunflower

orchid

pansy

poppy

tulip

petunia

rose

violet

197

Words for Fruits

apple

blackberry

blueberry

date

apricot

cantaloupe

grape

banana

cherry

grapefruit

kumquat

peach

plum

lemon

pear

raspberry

strawberry

orange

pineapple

watermelon

199

Words for Vegetables

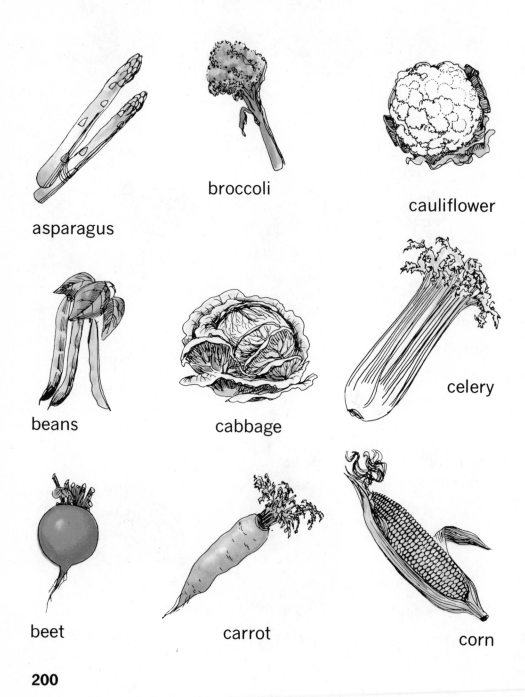

asparagus

broccoli

cauliflower

beans

cabbage

celery

beet

carrot

corn

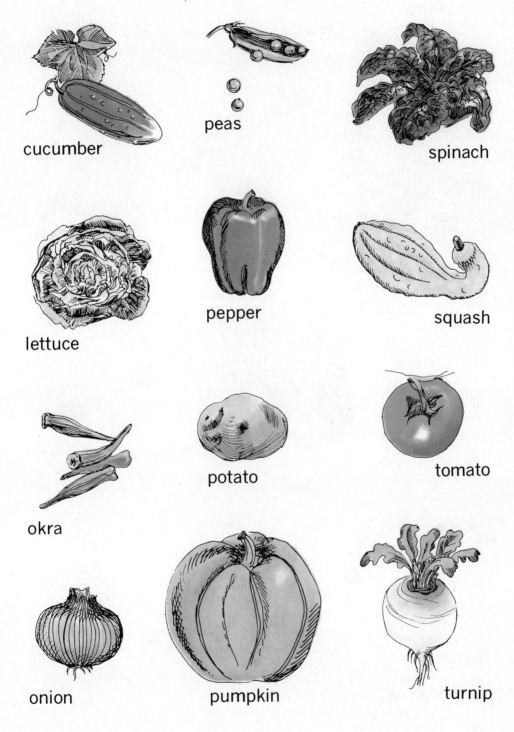

cucumber

peas

spinach

lettuce

pepper

squash

okra

potato

tomato

onion

pumpkin

turnip

201

Words for Animals

alligator

bat

bee

ant

bear

beetle

antelope

beaver

See **Birds,** page 211.

bird

buffalo

camel

chimpanzee

butterfly

cat

chipmunk

calf

chicken

clam

cow

cricket

See **Dogs,**
page 214.

dog

deer

dolphin

coyote

donkey

crab

dinosaur

204

duck

fly

giraffe

elephant

goat

fox

fish

frog

goose

205

kangaroo

gorilla

hippopotamus

grasshopper

hornet

kitten

hamster

horse

ladybug

lizard

mosquito

lamb

lobster

mouse

leopard

lion   monkey   octopus

207

rat

pony

opossum

puppy

rhinoceros

penguin

rabbit

seal

pig

raccoon

shark

208

snake

sheep

spider

swan

skunk

tiger

snail

squirrel

toad

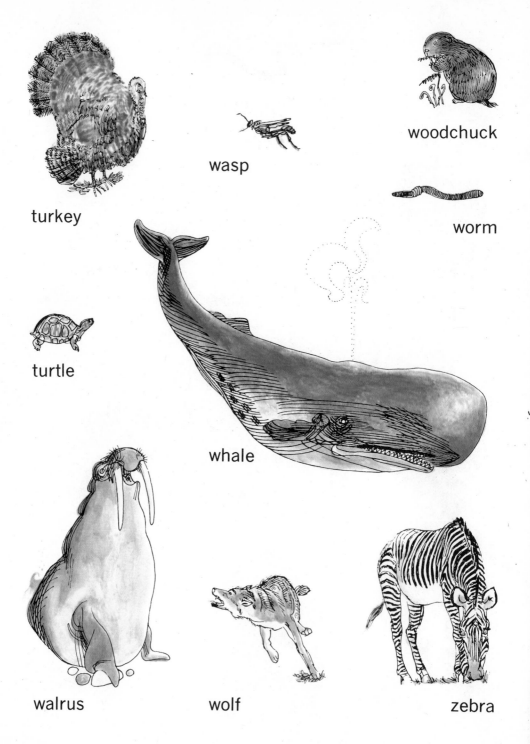

turkey

wasp

woodchuck

worm

turtle

whale

walrus

wolf

zebra

Birds

bluebird

cardinal

eagle

blue jay

chickadee

goldfinch

canary

crow

gull

mockingbird

parakeet

hawk

oriole

parrot

hummingbird

owl

parrot

meadowlark

peacock

212

pheasant

robin

whippoorwill

pigeon

sparrow

woodpecker

roadrunner

thrasher

wren

Dogs

Basset Hound

Bulldog

Collie

Beagle

Chihuahua

Dachshund

Boxer

Cocker Spaniel

Dalmatian

German Shepherd

Husky

Saint Bernard

Great Dane

Pointer

Setter

Greyhound

Poodle

Sheepdog

Words for Colors

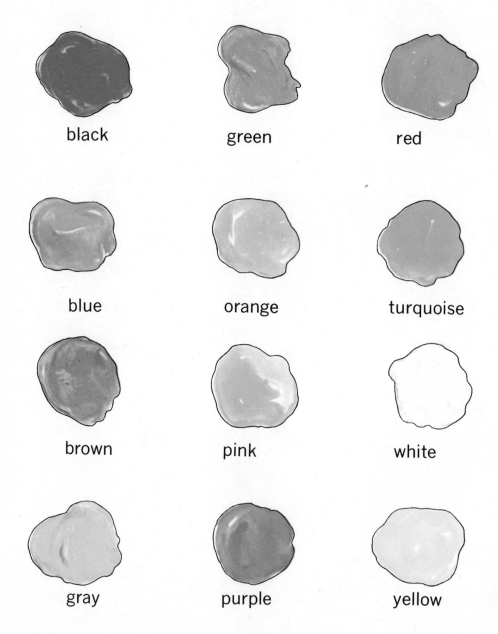

black   green   red

blue   orange   turquoise

brown   pink   white

gray   purple   yellow

Number Words

1	one	first		7	seven	seventh
2	two	second		8	eight	eighth
3	three	third		9	nine	ninth
4	four	fourth		10	ten	tenth
5	five	fifth		11	eleven	eleventh
6	six	sixth		12	twelve	twelfth

The Days of the Week

Sunday	Sun.	Thursday	Thurs.
Monday	Mon.	Friday	Fri.
Tuesday	Tues.	Saturday	Sat.
Wednesday	Wed.		

The Months and Some Important Days

January	February	March
Jan.	Feb.	Mar.
New Year's Day	Lincoln's Birthday Valentine's Day Washington's Birthday	St. Patrick's Day

April	May	June
Apr.		
	Mother's Day	Father's Day

July	August	September
	Aug.	Sept.
Fourth of July		

October	November	December
Oct.	Nov.	Dec.
Halloween	Thanksgiving Day	Christmas

To Parents and Teachers

MY SECOND PICTURE DICTIONARY has been designed to help the child learn more about the words he uses everyday. The words in the dictionary were selected on the basis of word studies by Horn, Rinsland, and Buckingham-Dolch. Another important source was the authors' study of high-frequency words from the compositions of primary-grade children. The contents and format of the book have been planned to offer the child opportunity to develop basic dictionary skills while expanding his understanding of language.

The first part of the book presents 1060 alphabetically-arranged entry words with definitions and illustrative sentences. Over one-half of the entries have full-color pictures to expand the child's understanding of the words. Throughout, there is a close correlation between the definition, the sentences, and the illustration for each entry word.

Most of the entry words are divided into syllables. The syllables indicate where a word can be divided at the end of a line in writing. If a word should not be divided because of a one-letter syllable at the beginning or end, it is shown solid (e.g. **about**). Stress marks are used as aids to pronunciation. The stress mark is not used, however, if the stressed syllable should not be written separately (e.g. **usu al**).

Many entry words have subentries to show how a word may change in form. The plural form of a noun is given as a subentry if it is formed in a way other than by adding *s*. The forms of a verb are given as subentries if they are not regularly formed. Other subentries include some common adjectives that are formed from nouns (e.g. **muddy**) and adverbs that are derived from adjectives (e.g. **gently**). Through such presentations, the child develops an understanding of the changes in forms of word classes as he examines these inflectional endings and suffixes.

When a word frequently serves as more than one part of speech, each meaning is indicated by a blue dot. To provide the child with a consistent pattern, noun definitions are given before verb definitions for multi-meaning entries.

In addition to the entries with definitions, nearly 200 cross-references are included in the main part of the dictionary. These cross-references help the child to locate the main forms of words, such as the irregular past tense verbs (e.g. **ate** *See* **eat.**) and commonly used irregular noun plurals (e.g. **men** *See* **man.**). Other cross-references direct the child to the illustrated word lists for animals, flowers, fruits, and vegetables at the back of the dictionary.

The word lists for MY SECOND PICTURE DICTIONARY show the child how words can be classified, since they are subject-centered. Included are antonyms, homonyms, compound words, and words for the space age. There are pages for the days of the week, the months and some important days, number words, colors, and kinds of workers. The classification lists are heavily illustrated to aid the child in learning more about the words.

EFGHIJK 079
PRINTED IN THE UNITED STATES OF AMERICA

WITHDRAWN FROM
JUNIATA COLLEGE LIBRARY